Penguin Books
WOMEN AND THE ARTS IN NEW ZEALAND

Elizabeth Eastmond is a lecturer in Art History at Auckland
University where she teaches courses on Renaissance art, r
book illumination and women and the arts. She is an arts
practitioner, and an occasional art writer. She was born in
England in 1945, studied Fine Arts at Edinburgh College of
at Edinburgh University and emigrated to New Zealand in 1￼
lives in Auckland.

Merimeri Penfold is a senior lecturer in Maori Language at
Auckland University where she also teaches a course in Maori
weaving and plaitwork. She was born in Te Hapua in 1924 and is
of Ngati Kurii-Te Aupouri descent. Merimeri Penfold is a member
of the New Zealand Council of Educational Research, of the Maori
Language Advisory Committee to the Education Department and
was chairwoman of the Management of Te Hapua 42 Incorporation.
She is a writer and also a translater of children's books and
manuscript material. She has five children, five grand-children and
lives in Auckland.

WOMEN AND THE ARTS
IN NEW ZEALAND
FORTY WORKS: 1936–86

Chosen and Introduced
by

Elizabeth Eastmond
and
Merimeri Penfold

Penguin Books

Penguin Books (N.Z.) Ltd, 182–190 Wairau Road, Auckland 10, New Zealand
Penguin Books Ltd, Harmondsworth, Middlesex, England
Penguin Books, 40 West 23rd Street, New York, New York 10010, U.S.A.
Penguin Books Australia Ltd, Ringwood, Victoria, Australia
Penguin Books Canada Ltd, 2801 John Street, Markham, Ontario, Canada L3R 1B4

First published by Penguin Books 1986
Copyright © 1986 Elizabeth Eastmond and Merimeri Penfold
All rights reserved

A Shoal Bay Press book
Typeset by Glenfield Graphics Ltd
Printed in Hong Kong through
Bookprint Consultants, Wellington

ACKNOWLEDGMENTS

Besides the artists included in this selection, the private owners of a number of
the works, public art gallery staff and photographers in centres outside
Auckland, we owe special thanks to Michael Dunn, Francis Pound and Priscilla
Pitts for checking the text, and to Peter Hannken for photographing many of
the Auckland works.

We should also like to acknowledge the crucial importance of the women's
movement for the basic conception of this book and for many of the
perspectives adopted.

THE MID-THIRTIES — the starting point for this selection — mark approximately the beginnings of the modern era in the history of Pakeha art in New Zealand. They also mark an important stage in the history of women artists in New Zealand.

The year in which 'art in this country made a new beginning' was how *Art in New Zealand* described 1936, for example.[1] That year witnessed the opening of the National Art Gallery, which besides providing a significant new context for the display of local work, also had the facilities to host such important exhibitions of overseas art as the exhibitions of Chinese art in 1937 and Canadian art in 1938. The crucial if conservative magazine *Art in New Zealand*, first published in 1928, was already well established; a splinter group of the Canterbury Society of Arts, the Group, was flourishing, and a similar offshoot of the Arts Society in Auckland, the Rutland Group, held its first exhibition in 1936. Both groups were numerically dominated by women.

These years saw the development of the notion of a national identity in the arts, which found major expression in the Centennial celebrations and exhibitions of 1940. In the sphere of painting, the careers of three major artists began during this period: Colin McCahon, M.T. Woollaston and Rita Angus, who was to become this country's most distinguished regional realist. Around this time she completed the distinctive 'Self-portrait' (Plate 3, Dunedin Art Gallery) which, in its projection of the look of the modern urban(e) young woman, distinguishes her generation from an older generation of women artists such as Margaret Stoddart and Dorothy Kate Richmond, both of whom were still working in the early thirties but who died in 1934 and 1935 respectively.

Other women artists besides Rita Angus had embarked on their careers in or by the thirties. There was Eve Polson (later Page) and Olivia Spencer-Bower; Louise Henderson had launched her long and still highly productive career, while Lois White was painting important works of allegory and social comment such as 'The War Makers' (1937, Auckland City Art Gallery). When Flora Scales returned to New Zealand in 1934 she passed on some valuable

insights gained at the Hans Hoffmann School in Munich to Toss Woollaston, and in 1939 May Smith returned from England to produce some of the most innovative work in the context of New Zealand art in the early forties.

During the thirties women painters were in a central and influential position within the small provincial setting of Pakeha New Zealand art, thus contradicting any anticipated pat formula of development from, say, thirties marginalisation to eighties prominence. Rita Angus, was producing highly significant works throughout the thirties and forties, as was New Zealand's major expatriate artist, Frances Hodgkins. Women painters did not enjoy the same strong showing in subsequent decades until the later seventies and eighties, although it is interesting to note that the first professional dealer gallery in New Zealand — complete with yellow ceiling, mats especially imported from Samoa, and custom-built furniture — was opened by a woman, Helen Hitchins, and operated in Wellington in the late forties and early fifties.

The artists mentioned above, however, are painters and it is important to remember that there is often a rather different tale to tell of women's contributions to other media: in fibre arts women, both Maori and Pakeha — for example Rangimarie Hetet, Puti Rare, Zena Abbott, Judy Wilson — have displayed a consistently high profile. In photography women photographers such as Ans Westra and Marti Friedlander were important in the fifties and sixties (they still are) and different branches of this medium are currently strongly represented by women such as Ann Noble, Gil Hanly, Christine Webster, Megan Jenkinson and Merylyn Tweedie. Molly Macalister and Alison Duff were major figures in post-war sculpture in New Zealand, and during the seventies and eighties, women artists such as Marté Szirmay, Christine Hellyar and Maria Olsen have provided key contributions to sculpture, with artists like Di Ffrench, Pauline Rhodes, Jacqueline Fraser and the younger Debra Bustin similarly influential in performance and installation. Among printmakers, earlier women representatives included Hilda Wiseman and Lois White, with a strong showing in more recent years from Kate Coolahan, Vivian Lynn, Marilyn Webb, Robin White and Carole Shepheard.

In *Two Hundred Years of New Zealand Painting* Gil Docking sympathetically noted how 'in our time and for sociological reasons with which everyone must surely be familiar, the traditional role of women in society is being reshaped. The outcome means that female energies of vast potentialities are now being released from domesticity into all areas of creative thinking and action'. There certainly has been a significant outpouring of women's creativity during the seventies and eighties — but has it been adequately reflected in our general books on the arts? And what of the contribution of the other women artists noted in this brief survey? Docking's book was published in 1971 and so predates the particularly productive (for both men and women artists) last fifteen years, and like Gordon Brown and Hamish Keith's *An Introduction to New Zealand Painting 1839–1980* (1969, revised 1982) it focuses only on the medium of painting, as do other texts. The latter book includes nine chapters on individual artists, none women (although the omission of a chapter on Rita Angus was beyond the authors' control). There is no mention of Lois White and in the revised edition, the ratio of women painters to men painters mentioned in the seventies update chapter is 8:48. Not surprisingly there is no mention of the beginnings of the women's art movement in New Zealand nor of any of the several exhibitions of women artists' work held in the seventies, one of which was *New Zealand's Women Painters* at the Auckland City Art Gallery, curated by Ann Kirker and Eric Young in 1975 to mark International Women's Year.

Women artists still occasionally suffer discrimination by being omitted from major general shows and survey texts. Most other obstacles — such as lack of access to nude models when history painting was a major genre; lack of access to guilds and academies; society's rigid and entrenched attitudes to the role of women in society, not to mention the very real obstacles of internalised attitudes regarding correct 'feminine behaviour' dating back to the development of the cult of femininity in the eighteenth and nineteenth centuries — do not apply any more. And such attitudes as selflessness, modesty and service (to men) — precisely those qualities which would effectively militate against the potential

young woman artist becoming a serious artist — no longer apply as they once did. Although remnants of that tradition did perhaps linger on in the documented attitudes of a number of historical New Zealand women artists such as May Smith and Flora Scales, both of whom, it appears, were extremely modest and exhibited their work rather infrequently, or Gabrielle Hope, who had to be encouraged to exhibit at all.

Although New Zealand was the first country to extend the franchise to women in 1893 it is interesting to note that society's attitudes remained out of step and exclusive in certain areas of the arts. For instance, women were not admitted to the Auckland Photographic Society until 1917,[2] and attitudes could be extremely oppressive in other situations. Society's prudery had a disastrous effect on at least two women artists' work: Edith Collier, who worked in Europe and returned to parochial Wanganui in the early twenties, had many of her nude studies destroyed by her father, as did Manawatu artist Elizabeth Berry in the forties.

In the past (and not-so-distant past), potential women artists have often had to make the choice, outlined relatively recently by English artist Carel Weight,[3] between making art 'at the end of the day when the husband has been fed and the children put to bed' or 'going to live in a convent' (his example is Gwen John), 'where the burdens of matrimony and the insecurities of spinsterhood were removed . . .' The choice, in other words, was between fulfilling society's expectations of women's primary role as nurturer and becoming a 'fulfilled *woman*', and making art a peripheral activity practised under conditions unlikely to further a career[4] or, on the other hand, choosing to place *art* at the centre of a 'necessarily' isolating lifestyle, where society's mores limited women's enjoyment of the social and sexual experience permitted men (and sometimes seen as necessary to the making of important art). Surely this dichotomy must have been evident to the several historical New Zealand women artists who placed painting at the centre of their lives and remained single — Frances Hodgkins, Rita Angus (married for four years only), Dorothy Kate Richmond, Margaret Stoddart, Grace Joel, Lois White, Flora Scales and Edith Collier.

On the plus side, one advantage which some middle-class historical women artists in New Zealand did enjoy was society's acceptance of them as 'unemployed' gentlewomen who, as a result of a pension or annuity (Flora Scales for example, and also Rita Angus for part of her career) were able to consistently pursue their involvement in art. (It was generally considered unmanly for a Pakeha man not to work in earlier New Zealand society.) Not that this situation absolved the women, however, from other gender-related problems such as isolation, which both Scales and Angus experienced as serious single women artists. Interestingly — and predictably, in the context of recent changes in social attitudes and social practice — the biographies of many of the women in this selection born during or after the Second World War show a variety of lifestyles; there are some single women, some married women artists, as well as a number of women artists who sucessfully manage to combine children *and* a husband or partner who is also an artist. Still, some might envy the position described for himself by Toss Woollaston after his marriage to Edith Alexander in 1936: 'She believed in my work, she lived with me in conditions considered sub-standard at the time, she mothered our four children, providing for me a full life. She was always available as a model in the evenings or whenever else I had any spare time . . .'[5]

It is instructive to substitute the male pronoun for 'she' and consider what stage of development the supportive *male* muse is at today.

But with or without male (or female) muses there is no doubt that women of all groups in New Zealand — Maori, Pacific Island, and Pakeha — are currently playing a vital role in all spheres of the arts despite one major lack — employment in substantial numbers in public gallery work and in tertiary arts education. The recognition and contribution of Pacific Island women is now being enriched through such efforts as those of a group of Tongan women led by Luseane Koloi who are reviving and teaching young women the art of *ngatu* — Tongan tapa making. An increasing number of Maori women besides those of long-standing importance like Rangimarie Hetet and her daughter Diggeress Te Kanawa, included in this selection, continue their involvement in traditional arts. Others, using modern media, have ranged in imagery from celebration of Maori values and traditions (Robyn Kahukiwa) to passionate and

forceful criticism of the dominant white culture in Aotearoa (Emily Karaka). Many Pakeha women artists are working effectively and successfully in a largely gender-neutral mode, among them Ingrid Banwell, Maria Olsen, Gretchen Albrecht, Pauline Thompson, Julia Morison, Pauline Rhodes, and other younger artists. Other women artists have for a number of years participated in the small but lively Women's Art Movement in this country: Allie Eagle (in its early stages); Juliet Batten — who has been a central figure as lecturer on women artists, facilitator of feminist collaborative projects and arts practitioner; Carole Shepheard, Merylyn Tweedie, Marion Evans, Bridie Lonie, Anna Keir, Claudia Pond Eyley — all involved in the establishment of the Women's Gallery, Wellington, 1980 — among many others. They have incorporated their feminism in the iconography of their work, in their approaches to art practice and by the questioning of certain established art-world notions, for example the arts/craft dichotomy[6], and they have challenged the until recently largely formalist approach in New Zealand art writing — the direction of the latter strategy linking their interests with a strand of post-modernism.

In 1986 several exhibitions of Maori women's art (both traditional and modern) were held at various centres; an exhibition of contemporary Maori art (incorporating work by men and women artists) travelled to Australia; and in 1985 a gender-balanced selection of New Zealand work was made for *ANZART* at the Sydney *Perspecta*. These are both indicators of and contributing factors towards the currently much-improved position of women in the arts in New Zealand.

In a book limited to forty images with only a brief text, the decision to represent a number of media as well as to attempt to present a cross-cultural selection has inevitably resulted in the omission of many important artists. The focus on image has also led to the omission of feminist collaborative projects which have concentrated on process and education; and this (European) emphasis on isolated art objects devoid of context makes it equally difficult to capture the integral sense of process, sociability and function in traditional Maori and other Polynesian arts. Our ratio of Maori and Pacific Island works to Pakeha is based roughly on population ratios, which at the last census (1981) rated Pacific Islanders

2.9 per cent, Maori 9.7 per cent and Pakeha 87.4 per cent. Other books on women currently in preparation have their different viewpoints and time frames.

We hope that this selection — with its inevitable mix of predictable and personal choices — will together with the other publications begin to reflect the vitality and diversity of women's cultural production in New Zealand/ Aotearoa.

Elizabeth Eastmond

MAORI WOMEN are currently in the midst of a dynamic movement of identification with aspects of our culture which urban Maori in particular have neglected for the past thirty or forty years. Women artists both traditional and modern have emerged from this context of the general revival of Maori cultural identity, with its growing awareness of the need to preserve and revive the language, the role of the marae and the culture as a whole. Their works have appeared in the settings of Maori communities, at local, regional and national hui and in public exhibitions of various kinds.

There is no doubt that during the depression years in the thirties — the starting point of this selection — as well as during World War II and the years of Maori urbanisation during the fifties, Maori women experienced great social changes which were often extremely detrimental to their sense of cultural identity and to their arts practice. In response the Maori Women's Welfare League was established in 1954. Though principally engaged in social issues such as housing, health and education, it was also a vital force in promoting a revival of Maori women's arts — a revival which is the basis of today's widespread renaissance of women's arts.

Despite this revival, the status and the wider recognition of women's traditional arts — the making of tukutuku, kete, piupiu, whariki, korowai, taniko, etc — has suffered from the Pakeha notion of the arts/crafts hierarchy, resulting in the frequent marginalisation of women's work in books and at exhibitions of Maori art. General books like Barrow's *Maori Art of New Zealand* (1978) focus on carving by men, while Brake, McNeish and Simmons's chapter headed 'New Zealand' in *Arts and Artists of Oceania* (1983, eds. Mead and Kernot) has only two illustrations of women's art. The major exhibition *Te Maori*, travelling centres in America 1985/6 does not feature any women's art.

In traditional Maori society art and life were intertwined. The cultural production of men (largely carving) and of women (mainly fibre arts) were both highly regarded and were both accompanied by ritual and tapu to become an integral part of that most significant complex of cultural and artistic expression, the whare whakairo.

Recent exhibitions of traditional women's arts such as the important *Feathers and Fibre*, Rotorua Art Gallery, 1984, have done a great deal to counter biases like those mentioned above and to enhance the reputations of these arts. Among several other exhibitions of Maori art, 1986 has seen the organisation of three simultaneous exhibitions of Maori women's art under the overall title *Karanga Karanga* at The Fisher Gallery, Pakuranga, the Gisborne Museum and Arts Centre, and the City Art Gallery, Wellington. At the Fisher Gallery works ranged from the traditional kakahu made by Puti Hineaupounamu Rare, to Maureen Lander's installation involving muka and plastic; from Katerina Mataira's composition of a waiata especially for the exhibition, to paintings in a contemporary expressionist style by Kura Irirangi Rewiri-Thorsen. This inclusive approach challenges most Pakeha notions of art gallery exhibition practice and certainly events like these, with their focus on innovative modern works as well as traditional arts, promise an exciting future in Aotearoa for Maori women working in the arts.

Merimeri Penfold

1 'Ourselves', *Art in New Zealand*, Vol IX, No. 2, Dec 1936, p.63.

2 Walker, Tim. 'Margaret Matilda White, Photographer, 1868–1910', p.1. Research essay, 1982.

3 'Jean Bratby', *Motif*, Winter 1963–64, 86–88.

4 Of the several to whom this applies, two examples: Frances Hodgkins's sister Isobel, initially considered to be the more promising of the two, who gave up serious painting after her marriage; and Anne Hamblett, promising fellow student and later wife of Colin McCahon.

5 From a text accompanying a display of Woollaston works at the Rotorua Art Gallery, 1986.

6 The Wellington Women's Fabric Art Company's touring *Stuffed Stuff* exhibition, 1984, is one example.

PLATE 1

Zena Abbott was born in Auckland in 1922 and first studied textile weaving with Ilse von Randow in 1952 at the Auckland City Art Gallery. Although she is best known as one of New Zealand's major fibre artists, throughout her career she has also studied drawing and painting, and from 1973–75 attended classes held by Gretchen Albrecht and James Ross. In 1958 she opened the first professional handweaving studio in New Zealand at Blockhouse Bay, Auckland, where she operated a cottage industry, taught and employed numerous women and supplied galleries and craft shops all over New Zealand. In 1959 she became interested in extending the traditional boundaries of weaving into three-dimensional fibre constructions. She has exported to Australia and has exhibited throughout New Zealand and also in Australia, England, Canada and America. In 1976 she received the Kohn Award and in 1985 a major retrospective of her work was shown at the Fisher Gallery, Pakuranga.

Zena Abbott has occasionally woven other artists' designs, for example those of May Smith and Louise Henderson, works by whom appear in this selection: see Plates 33 and 14. In her own work she has been concerned with presenting her often highly sculptural fibre works in an art rather than a craft context, sometimes working on a very large scale as in a four-panel hanging at Rutherford High School, Auckland, 1978, or in 'Opus 6' (1976–77, Fisher Art Gallery, Pakuranga) a monumental circular work (weight 36kg). She uses both natural and analine dyes (helped in the dyeing process by Colin Watson) and has experimented with a wide range of materials ranging from flax fibre through art silk to alkathene piping and burglar alarm tape.

'Scrolls' is a large-scale installation piece which is both ceremonial and warmly accessible in character. The artist says she likes to construct 'an inviting environment', and here she presents the spectator with the intriguing option of unrolling the scrolls which gradually reveal a text woven into them: 'From thorny plants the hidden fibre', alluding to the cactus plant sisal which provides her with a favourite material and one used in the 'Scrolls' themselves.

PLATE 2

Gretchen Albrecht was born in Auckland in 1943, studied at Elam School of Fine Arts, University of Auckland, and apart from a number of study trips to the USA, Europe and Australia, continues to work mainly in Auckland. From 1972–73 she was Teaching Fellow in Painting at Elam, and in 1981 Frances Hodgkins Fellow at the University of Otago, Dunedin. Albrecht has exhibited widely in New Zealand and in 1985 took part in the NZ/NY painting exhibition in New York. She is married to the painter James Ross and has one son.

Although primarily a painter, Albrecht has also worked with fabric (a felt mural commission for Auckland University School of Medicine 1975) and has designed banners: for the opera Tristan and Iseult, 1978 and for Hotspur, a commission from the Ministry of Foreign Affairs in 1980.

Besides the example of Frances Hodgkins, Albrecht cites as an early crucial influence the teaching of American art history lecturers Arthur Lawrence and Kurt von Meier — the former for his enthusiasm for the Romanesque and Renaissance periods, the latter for introducing her to the work of artists such as Paula Modersohn-Becker and Sonia Delaunay-Terk. They conveyed the notion, she says, that 'our inheritance as artists and scholars was not to be confined to local, regional or national concerns, but was inextricably bound up with the rest of the world'. This nicely articulates the International Modernist background to Albrecht's work. Since 1981 Albrecht has been using hemispherical canvasses, painted increasingly expressively in her characteristically brilliant and highly sensuous palette. These works demonstrate a complex and individual integration of classic form (the arch/ lunette-like shape of the canvasses), late Modernism (the self-signifying paintwork) and an intentionally evocative and arguably Post-Modernist choice of titles ('Response', 'Radiant', 'Giotto's Blue', 'Luna' . . .) 'Exile' is similarly highly allusive and was painted as one of four canvasses for an Artist's Project exhibition entitled 'Seasonal'/Four Paintings at the Auckland City Art Gallery December 1985–March 1986.

PLATE 3

Rita Angus was born in Hastings in 1908 and studied at Canterbury College School of Art. Although now generally regarded as this country's most outstanding Regionalist, her reputation became firmly established only in 1983–84 when a major touring retrospective of her work took place. She was forty-nine when she had her first one-woman exhibition. She died in 1970.

Rita Angus lived and worked in both the South Island and the North Island, settling in a cottage in Thorndon, Wellington in 1953. She was married between 1930 and 1934 to the painter Alfred Cook. A pacifist, during the war years she refused the Industrial Manpower's directive to work for a Christchurch rubber manufacturer and while in Wellington in 1942 completed the well-known portrait 'Betty Curnow' (Auckland City Art Gallery). 1949–50 saw her health decline (in 1949 she was admitted to a psychiatric hospital), but she continued to paint, took part in group exhibitions and in 1958–59 travelled to England and Europe on a New Zealand Art Society's Fellowship. Back in Wellington she lived at times under frugal conditions. In 1965 she contributed to the Queen Elizabeth II Arts Council exhibition of New Zealand painting in London and in 1969 to a similar exhibition at the Smithsonian Institute, Washington.

In an artist's statement of 1947, her aims, she wrote, include 'As a woman painter (to) represent love of humanity and faith in mankind in a world which is to me, richly variable and infinitely beautiful . . . (and to) . . . create a living freedom from the afflicting theme of death.'

The artist's work ranges from exquisitely delicate watercolours of flowers through what have come to be seen (to the Pakeha) as archetypal images of the New Zealand landscape, to surrealist imagery, and includes a large number of compelling portraits. She painted many self-portraits at different stages in her life and experimented with this genre by imaging herself in various roles, for instance as 'Cleopatra' in 1938, or as 'Rutu', 1951 (both Rita Angus Loan Collection, National Art Gallery) with brown Polynesian skin and blonde hair, symbolising an optimistic melding of the two cultures. In the very 'thirties' 'Self-portrait' (pictured), the artist presents herself as an assured woman gazing out at the viewer/herself with an expression of uncompromising directness.

PLATE 4

Ingrid Banwell was born in Taupo in 1957. She was educated at schools in Mexico City, Wellington and New York and graduated M.F.A. from Auckland University School of Fine Arts in 1981. In 1985 Banwell was awarded a major Queen Elizabeth II Arts Council Travel Grant which she will use in 1986 for study in the USA. While working in part-time jobs as art tutor and librarian assistant, she has been able to maintain a continuity of work and has exhibited regularly in group and one-woman shows.

Banwell's recent work has been mainly concerned with painted wall constructions where she has experimented with the dividing line between painting and sculpture, with the polarities of geometric and organic shapes, and, in her own words, with 'assimilating both Oceanic and European art forms in an endeavour to create an art form that reflects the multi-cultural influences we are exposed to'. Her recent constructions have been characterised by a larger scale and by a greater three-dimensionality. Banwell is an admirer of the work of contemporary artists such as Elizabeth Murray and Frank Stella, and, within the New Zealand context, Gordon Walters, Robert Jesson and Richard Killeen. An interesting and amusing aspect of her work is her use of titles which have frequently referred to the rather pompous and moralising tone adopted by certain writing in the popular media, and especially that found in gardening manuals (she is a keen gardener), for example, 'Taming that Uncontrollable Habit', 'Dealing with those Untidy Edges', 'Garden Grooming'. In 'An Indigenous Spring Specimen' the use of moving parts — the cork elements at the top, for example — was, she says, 'an endeavour to bind together a more varied use of materials with a more whimsical approach to the pieces. It also extended the work more into the spectator space, and gave it a more animated quality'. This work was crucial in Banwell's development from a more two-dimensional approach towards working in a more explicitly three-dimensional manner.

PLATE 5

Philippa Blair was born in Christchurch in 1945, studied Fine Arts at Canterbury University and has exhibited regularly in group and one-woman shows in New Zealand since 1969. She has also exhibited in Brisbane, New York and San Francisco, worked as an art teacher in Australia and New Zealand and as a graphic designer in Australia. Blair has been a frequent traveller to Europe and America, where she has worked, and in 1984 was awarded a Queen Elizabeth II Arts Council Grant to take up an Artist in Residence scheme at the Canberra School of Art. In 1985 she was Visiting Lecturer in Painting at Canterbury University School of Fine Arts. She has two teenage daughters, is currently based in Auckland and is also involved in music, dance and theatre.

Important early influences cited by Blair include the teaching of Rudolf Gopaz, the work of Kandinsky, the New Zealand-born artist Len Lye, as well as de Kooning and Pollock.

From 1981 Philippa Blair has become well-known for her exuberantly painted, folded canvasses — her *Cloak* and *Heart/Book* series — whose flaps and layers can sometimes be rearranged by the viewer. Works like 'Morning Star Tipi' (1982, private collection) and 'South Island Mountain Cloak' (1985, Robert McDougall Art Gallery, Christchurch) fall into this category. An interest of Blair's expressed in these works is that of the enveloping, shelter-shape of house, tent, *tipi* or korowai.

Blair has also worked in other media including print-making and stained glass. In 1983 she designed a window for the Cook Island Church, Otara. The design of 'Queen of Hearts' — with its extremely vivid coloured glass and lively brushmarks — cleverly combines the outline of the structure of her *Cloak* series with that of the *Heart* series. The Queen, who Blair describes as 'quite a character' winks her eye in the left segment of the heart.

PLATE 6

Kate Coolahan was born in 1929 in Sydney and moved to New Zealand in 1952 where she has been employed as a graphic designer and was the first woman lecturer in the Design School at Wellington Polytechnic. She has been a key figure in New Zealand art education, has been elected to numerous boards in conjunction with the arts and has received several awards, most recently a Queen Elizabeth II Award to exhibit and lecture at the World Print Council in San Francisco in 1985. In 1984 she was invited artist and special prize-winner at the Premi Internazionale Biella (Italy). Kate Coolahan has made two study trips to Japan and has exhibited regularly both in New Zealand and internationally (for example at the 1972 Venice Biennale, and at major print biennials). A major retrospective of her work is currently touring the country (1985–86).

Developing in the fifties, a time in New Zealand Coolahan remembers for its scarcity of artists' materials and its cultural poverty, the artist's work has been characterised by its diversity: besides painting and print-making (Coolahan was one of the first artists to use photo-etching in New Zealand), she has pioneered paper-making, has worked in fibre (making several tufted carpets), plastics, assemblage and situational sculpture. This variety, she stresses, is 'expressive not of not being able to make up your mind, it's about acknowledging different needs and finding a way for them to co-exist'. She has been interested in works by artists such as Sol le Witt, Rauschenberg and Eva Hesse. Throughout her career, including the years of her marriage (her husband died in 1985), Kate Coolahan has been a consistent advocate of women's economic and social independence. She is an enthusiastic gardener.

Social concerns such as communication and immigration have featured in Coolahan's work ('Immigrant Women in the Wairarapa', 1979, 'Victoria in the Pacific' 1976), as have complexities of modes of perception in a number of works on the theme of filters: 'Filters' 1974, an assemblage work combining found objects with imagery painted by the artist, is an example. This work was exhibited in the Wellington 1974 conceptual sculpture exhibition *In Mind*, probably the first exhibition of its kind in New Zealand.

PLATE 7

Bronwynne Cornish was born in Wellington in 1945. She worked with the potter Helen Mason in the Waitakeres from 1968–70 and from 1971–78 worked on Waiheke Island when she moved into the sphere of ceramic sculpture. Now one of New Zealand's major sculptors, she has received a number of awards, most recently a Queen Elizabeth II Arts Council grant to travel to Italy and Britain (1984). Also in 1984 she was Artist in Residence at Tangaroa College, Otara and in 1985 a Visiting Tutor at the Otago School of Ceramics. She lives in Auckland with her husband artist Denys Watkins and her two teenage daughters and is a keen gardener.

Cornish's larger-scale works like 'Subterranean Desert' (1980, Dowse Art Gallery, Lower Hutt), 'Home is where the Heart is' (1983, also Dowse Art Gallery), and 'Dedicated to the Kindness of Mothers' (1983) share with an international stream of art-making a concern with aspects of the art of prehistory.

The ancient earth mother-like figure of 'Dedicated to the Kindness of Mothers' (the original title of her 'Garden Mother' when she was shown at Auckland City Art Gallery, 1983–84) was originally surrounded on the gallery walls by clay skull masks and accompanied by 'prehistoric' urns. Potentially a somewhat grim and eerie arrangement, Cornish's use of warm pink neon lighting over the masks, together with a strong shaft of light on the curious but smiling ceramic face of the figure, gave the installation a more positive and accessible character, an aspect which is enhanced by the work's present garden setting. Here the work continues in Cornish's life: she varies the planting seasonally and at the time this photograph was taken (February 1986) she was considering a winter planting of red cabbage and curly kale. Cornish has surrounded the figure with a grove of citrus which adds further to the rich range of associations evoked by this work.

PLATE 8

Claudia Pond Eyley was born in Matamata in 1946, attended schools in Montreal, Canada, and Yonkers, New York, before studying at Elam School of Fine Arts, Auckland University. Recent study travel abroad has included the USA and Mexico in 1980 and Kiribati in 1984, where she and her daughter Brigid stayed with the New Zealand artist Robin White. She has exhibited regularly since 1969 and from 1980 has also shown her work in a number of group exhibitions of feminist art. She has taken part in collaborative feminist performance and installation work and early in 1986 she shared a five-year survey show with Carole Shepheard at the Centre Gallery, Wellington.

Claudia Pond Eyley is Assistant Lecturer in Freehand Drawing at Auckland University's School of Architecture. She is married with two daughters and lives in Auckland.

Pond Eyley has been actively involved in the Women Artist's Movement and she is a member of VAANA (Visual Artists Against Nuclear Arms). In conjunction with these activities the artist has designed a large body of artwork, ranging from postcards to magazine covers and murals; she has also taken part in many panel discussions, seminars and given a number of lectures.

Her work has developed through a period of gestural abstract painting in the earlier seventies; through colourful, celebratory images of her domestic and garden environment to her current (from 1983) series of 'shield' collage/paintings. 'Shield Painting with ochre-black Surround' like others incorporates images of and by women from various periods and cultures: the theme of female ancestry, creativity and strength making these works powerfully feminist statements. Included here in photo-silkscreen are, for example: the prehistoric 'Venus of Willendorf'; a self-portrait by Mexican artist Frieda Kahlo; an early drawing by her daughter Lydia; and, interestingly, a replica in miniature of one of her own early 'shield' paintings.

PLATE 9

Jacqueline Fahey was born in 1930 in Timaru, graduated from Canterbury University in 1951 and first exhibited her work in 1952. Family commitments (including three daughters) have resulted in certain periods of her career being more productive artistically than others, but she has been able to work continuously since 1978. In the early sixties she co-organised a group show with Rita Angus at the Centre Gallery, Wellington — probably one of the first consciously 'gender-balanced' exhibitions in New Zealand. She moved with her husband and family to Auckland in 1965, and in 1980 received a Queen Elizabeth II Arts Council grant to travel to America to research the Women Artists Movement. In 1983 the City Gallery, Wellington organised a mini-retrospective of her painting. In 1984 she was a participant in the Auckland City Art Gallery's *Anxious Images* exhibition and in 1985 a New Zealand representative for the Australian *Perspecta* exhibition, Sydney.

For much of her career Jacqueline Fahey has worked in variants of an expressive realist style, focusing — in the years when this was deemed unfashionable, and more recently — on women's experience within the home, on family interactions including generational and marriage conflict ('Mother and Daughter Quarrelling', 1975, Robert McDougall Art Gallery, Christchurch, 'Drinking Couple, Fraser Analysing my Words', 1978, Auckland University School of Medicine), and self-image.

In 1981–82 Fahey 'moved out of the house'. 'Hill of Bitter Memories', set in the Auckland Domain (1981–82, private collection) is a powerful work from this phase which explores both Maori and Pakeha history. Tragedy, irony and a sharp wit (in various combinations) characterise many of Fahey's works. 'My Skirt's in Your Fucking Room!' humorously records the kind of distraction familiar to artists who are also mothers and the title takes a tilt at conventions of 'genteel' language. In the foreground is Ann Sutherland Harris and Linda Nochlin's *Women Artists: 1550–1950*, a crucial text in the drive during the seventies to rediscover and re-evaluate historical women artists. The work was painted for the touring theme show *Mothers* organised by the Women Artists' Gallery, Wellington in 1981.

PLATE 10
Di Ffrench was born in 1946 in Melbourne, Australia, and moved to New Zealand in 1963. Before 1976 she worked privately on performance and a series of art in the mail projects, then moved into public installation/ performance and sculpture. She continues her involvement in this area, although recent works (from 1984) have focused on the photograph as medium for her 'representation' of constructed objects and actions. She has presented performance/installation works in various New Zealand centres and also in the USA — Wisconsin in 1978 and 1979 — and in Australia ('Asters' at *ANZART* in Tasmania, 1983).

Di Ffrench is married to the sculptor Peter Nicholls and has four children. She travelled to Toronto to attend the tenth International Sculpture Conference in 1978, and within Canada and America from 1978–79. She lives in Dunedin.

Other major installation/performances include 'South Pacific Souvenir', 1980, a work protesting the dangers of pollution produced by the projected smelter at Aramoana (near Dunedin); 'Fontanel', for *ANZART*, Christchurch, 1981, and 'The Opinion', 1984. Involving a number of objects which the artist had made over a period of several months, plus film and a smokescreen, 'The Opinion' was a complex work raising questions about the nature of power structures and of critical opinion.

'The Useful Idiot and Arnolfini's Hat' is also a complex work conveying a range of notions: Ffrench stresses her interest in 'researching ideas' and in making works which ask questions. Here there are a number of effectively odd and thought-provoking disjunctions: they include the quotation from Lenin in the title, linked with Arnolfini's

hat from the famous fifteenth-century double portrait by Jan van Eyck and the substitution of the woman artist for the male merchant Arnolfini, a device of displacement/appropriation which can perhaps be read as a challenge to the notions of male power and the 'male gaze'.

PLATE 11
Jacqueline Fraser was born in Dunedin in 1956, studied at Elam School of Fine Arts, Auckland, from 1974–77 and has exhibited in a number of group shows in Australia and New Zealand including the Mildura Sculpture Triennial, 1978, the Sydney Biennale 1979, *ANZART* at Christchurch 1981 and Auckland 1985, and *Perspecta*, Sydney, 1986. She has had regular one-woman exhibitions in dealer galleries from 1978, when the installation 'Lunar Eclipse' was displayed at the Bosshard Gallery, Dunedin, and has also made several works for alternative spaces such as public parks (most recently Mount Eden, 1981) and restaurants and cafes (for example DKD in Auckland, 1985).

After graduating from Elam, Fraser moved back to Dunedin and then to Auckland in 1982. She has two children who attend a KohangaReo pre-school and is of Ngai Tahu descent.

Fraser works with light objects and materials, both natural (for example willow twigs) and artificial. She ties, weaves, stretches, plaits and scatters the component parts of her highly delicate constructions in the given space, creating fragile networks of fine lines and luminous small patches of colour.

As in other works, Fraser displays an extreme lightness of touch in these two details from 'Kauri Installation' (Sue Crockford Gallery), which together with their symmetry and the use of repeated knottings and tyings, can give the viewer a sense of witnessing the result of some private, almost magical ritual. The whole installation was constructed by Fraser at the gallery over a concentrated four-day work period from materials brought with her and from others, like the kauri planks, found nearby — an approach typical of her spontaneity and ingenuity.

PLATE 12
Matarena George was born in 1935 on Pukapuka, an atoll of the Cook Island group. She moved with her mother to Rarotonga to attend school, where her interest in art developed, although as a girl growing up in Cook Island society there was already the strong tradition of girls learning and practising skills like *tivaevae* (quilt or coverlet-making) taught by their mothers and other older female members of the family group. Matarena George's father was a tailor: she remembers watching him with interest as he cut patterns and chose materials. She took up nursing for a time, but maintained her interest in *tivaevae*, soon experimenting with her own designs, which she has continued to do throughout the years she has lived in New Zealand.

Mrs Matarena George is married with eight children

and lives in Auckland. She is a member of the cultural group *Pacifica* and she has taken part in a number of Pacific Island cultural gatherings, such as the annual Pacific Island Conferences. She stresses the richness and diversity of cultural production of the many different peoples within the Pacific and also the variety that can exist within one particular cultural group such as the Cook Islands, where there are many different traditions. She works consistently on her *tivaevae*, and also on crochet, smaller-scale embroidery on pillow-cases, woven hats and fans and the making of intricate cushion-covers. The *tivaevae* are usually made in collaboration with other women: the 'Pansy Tivaevae' for instance was worked on by a group of four women, one of whom was Mrs Naomi Tutini, a regular collaborator with Mrs George.

Although the concept of quilt-making was brought to the Cook Islands by early missionaries the women soon adapted and extended the imported skill by using a very different and particularly vivid colour range and developing new methods and designs, often based on local flora. Within Cook Island society *tivaevae* originally functioned as ceremonial objects, made for social events of especial significance like births, hair-cutting ceremonies, weddings, deaths. Now, *tivaevae* continue to be used for these occasions as well as for gifts, and are occasionally for sale to the public. They can often take up to a year to make.

Mrs Matarena George is currently conceiving a design for a series of fabric wall-hangings based on one of the Cook Island creation myths.

PLATE 13

Christine Hellyar was born in New Plymouth in 1947, and studied at Elam School of Fine Arts, Auckland University. From 1982 she has been a lecturer at Elam. She was awarded a Queen Elizabeth II Arts Council grant in 1976, has travelled extensively in Europe and North America and lived in Scotland in 1977. In 1985 she co-curated the *ANZART* Artists' Book Show with Carole Shepheard. She has exhibited in group and one-woman shows from the early seventies, participating in a number of international shows (for example the Sydney Biennale, 1982) and *ANZART* in Christchurch (1981) and Auckland (1985). She is married with one child and lives in Auckland. Among her special interests are the art of prehistory and visiting museums of natural history.

For much of her career Hellyar's work has drawn inspiration from natural forms, fauna and flora, sometimes using found natural objects such as rocks and feathers themselves as part of the work in conjunction with materials like plaster, lead, latex and, more recently, bronze. Titles are important in Hellyar's work and they can be poetic, punning or cryptic: 'Thought Cupboard: Enhancing'; 'Soft Jottings'; 'Low Creature Rears its Ugly Head'; 'Tame Cabbage Fans'. . . . Some works have been concerned with small shelter shapes, for instance 'Rock Nooks' (1981), and a major installation at Auckland City Art Gallery entitled 'Shelter' (1982) which effectively explored notions of the home or shelter as both refuge and trap.

'Tool Trays', originally displayed in one row flat on the gallery floor, has obvious connections with displays of prehistoric artefacts. A wide range of materials is used, often in surprising combinations: an 'axe' with feather accessory set in on a soft bed of felt, a heavy rock 'for Women's Roads' within a small round flax kete, made, like the felting, by the artist. These combinations together with the titles for each tray are characteristic of this artist's ingenuity and wit and point to some of the general connections between her work and that of women sculptors like Meret Oppenheim and Louise Bourgeoise.

PLATE 14

Louise Henderson was born in Paris in 1912, studied at Canterbury University School of Art, at Victoria University, and at Auckland University under John Weeks. Her father was secretary to Rodin and her grandfather was a Minister of the Arts in France. Returning to Paris in 1952, she studied under the neo-cubist painter Jean Metzinger. Back in New Zealand she had her first one-woman exhibition at the Auckland City Art Gallery in 1953. From 1955–58 she travelled in the Middle East, and exhibited in London in 1952 and 1956. Since 1959 she has exhibited regularly in New Zealand and has also had shows in Sydney, Brussels, Paris and in England. In 1973 she was awarded a Queen Elizabeth II Fellowship for her outstanding contribution to New Zealand painting.

Louise Henderson has also lectured in the arts: on creative embroidery and design at Canterbury; at Wellington Teachers' College; and in painting at Sydney and Auckland Universities. Her writings on the arts include articles on embroidery and tapestry in which she encouraged experimentation and called for a more serious consideration of these aspects of creativity as art forms.

Henderson's career has been distinguished by an extremely experimental approach to the use of a great variety of media and by a lively diversity of styles. She stresses the importance of the notion, the *idea* dictating choice of medium and style. Her well-known triptych 'The Lakes' (1965, Auckland City Art Gallery) is an important example of a lyrical abstract Expressionist phase in her work; 'Houses in Dieppe' (1959) (Plate 14 in Francis Pound's *Forty Modern New Zealand Paintings* in this series) is an example of work in geometric abstraction. She has also worked in stained glass, sculpture, mosaic, print-making and fibre. An interesting recurring motif in her *oeuvre* is the double-image of two women, a feature of a number of other women artists' work, for example Mary Cassatt and Frances Hodgkins.

'Still Life — Glass and Printed Cloth' involved the difficult technique of painting on the back of the glass so that no corrections or over-painting were possible. It is executed in a lively version of decorative late Cubism — a style radical and modern in the context of New Zealand painting around 1950.

PLATE 15

Rangimarie Hetet (neé Hursthouse) is Ngati Maniapoto and comes from Te Kuiti in the King Country, where she has lived all her life. She was born in 1892, learned weaving skills from her mother who had fought in the Waikato wars of the 1860s and continues to make the fine Maori garments for which she is renowned. She has been for many years the unchallenged authority in the traditional arts of raranga and whatu and during her lifetime has created and produced many fine mats and ceremonial garments for use at special Maori and Pakeha functions. A korowai such as that shown in Plate 15 would be worn by a woman to mark important occasions such as the tangi, weddings, or university graduation. For some years Rangimarie worked in isolation, particularly in the area of weaving, but she has been concerned in passing on her skills and knowledge to her daughter Diggeress and succeeding generations of her family. Her approach to her work is most professional. She considers all aspects of the item she has decided to create and before she begins has a clear idea of size, the amount of material required in terms of natural and dyed muka and the type of feathers to be used, such as kiwi and pigeon. Because these birds are protected special provisions have been made to enable Rangimarie and others to acquire feathers from museums and other sources. It is not until these aspects of the work are finalised in her mind that she begins work.

She is fastidious in all aspects of her art and the garment selected for this series is a manifestation of her mana as a recognised Maori woman artist at national and international level. Rangimarie Hetet has been the recipient of many awards, among them a Queen Elizabeth II Arts Council grant and the 1982 *Mediawomen* award for the arts.

PLATE 16

Frances Hodgkins was born in 1869 in Dunedin, where her father William Matthew Hodgkins was a solicitor and an influential painter and her sister a successful landscape painter until her marriage. Dunedin society was one where the emancipation of women was beginning to be felt: a number of women of Frances Hodgkins's generation were painters and in 1893 when Hodgkins studied under the Italian painter Nerli, women gained the vote in New Zealand (the first country to extend the franchise). Hodgkins also attended Dunedin School of Art and in 1901, feeling that she had 'not yet realised herself', she left New Zealand for the first of her three journeys to Europe. The second was in 1906 and the third and last in 1913. In Europe from 1906 she began to consolidate her career by exhibiting; she also taught classes at Colorossi's in Paris and later started her own school of watercolour painting for women. Her work at this time was primarily impressionist-oriented (for example 'The Hill Top' c. 1908, National Art Gallery, Wellington). Later the importance of the Post-Impressionists and Matisse can be seen in works like 'Double Portrait'

(c. 1922, Hocken Library, Dunedin), and it was not until 1929 (that is, when she was sixty) that she came to be regarded as among the front rank of the English avant-garde. This was marked by her election to the Seven and Five Society, a group which included artists such as Ben Nicholson and expatriate New Zealander Len Lye.

From the thirties came Hodgkins's distinctive series of still life-landscape combinations which she painted in an increasingly free and fluid style. The notorious 'Pleasure Garden' (c. 1933, Robert McDougall Art Gallery, Christchurch) is one of these: initially rejected by the Robert McDougall Gallery advisory committee in 1949, it was eventually gifted to the Gallery by members of the public. However in the forties in England her reputation was strong: Eric Newton called Frances Hodgkins 'the most original and individual painter in England today' (1940) and her status was reinforced that year through her selection as a British representative at the Venice Biennale. In 1946, a year before she died, a major retrospective of her work was held at the Lefevre Galleries, London, and in 1948 a monograph on Frances Hodgkins appeared in the Penguin Modern Painters series. In New Zealand, E.H. McCormick's writings and the 1969 Centenary Exhibition at the Auckland City Art Gallery were crucial to this country's recognition, reappraisal and 'reclaiming' of this most important of New Zealand's historical expatriate artists.

She worked consistently through the forties until a few months before her death in 1947 at a psychiatric hospital near Dorchester. 'Self-Portrait: Still Life', 1941, Auckland City Art Gallery (Pound, Plate 16) is an outstanding example of her late style. It is also a work which, interestingly, has been of importance to a number of more recent New Zealand women artists: to Gretchen Albrecht, for example, the work demonstrated 'how one could use metaphor in painting'. 'Zipp', a later almost abstract still life in more sombre colours, shares the motif of the shoe, its various other objects — with the organic cluster around the snake-like zip — spread out over the picture surface emphasising it to the edges in a rather innovative way for painting in Britain at this time.

PLATE 17

Gabrielle Hope was born in Lower Hutt in 1916, studied at Elam School of Fine Arts, and exhibited her work in a number of group shows in Auckland and Hamilton from 1946. In 1955 and 1957 she had one-woman exhibitions at the Auckland Society of Arts and at Argus House Gallery. She died at the age of forty-six in 1962. There have been three posthumous exhibitions at dealer galleries of Gabrielle Hope's work: in the mid-sixties, early seventies and most recently in 1983.

Hope's work was mainly executed in watercolour and gouache and is characterised by a lively spontaneity of approach, a lightness of touch and swiftly painted brushstrokes. There is a freshness about her perception and style which owes something to her interest in Chinese painting (for example 'Mangere Landscape', c. 1954, private collection). Her choice of subjects ranged from landscapes to still lifes to figures, portraits and animals. Some of these works reflect her strong interest in mysticism and in western and eastern occult traditions: 'Ancient Theme' (1953 Hocken Library, Dunedin) is a landscape-still life à la Hodgkins which includes a large amphora in the foreground; 'The Chariot', as described by Ross Fraser (*Art New Zealand* 30), incorporates references to Plato's *Phaedrus* and possibly to Tarot cards; 'The Tree' (Peter Shaw, Auckland) probably refers to the Tree of Life/the mystic tree of the East.

'The Poet (Self-portrait)' is a haunting image painted in a gestural style and with an expressive use of colour. It was completed in 1953, the year of her remarriage and move to Milford, a period which proved to be the beginning of a particularly productive phase in her work — aided also no doubt by the opportunities provided by the building of a studio.

Gabrielle Hope, in common with a number of other women artists: Gwen John, Grace Joel, Flora Scales and May Smith was, it seems, extremely modest about her work and reticent about showing it. This, together with the lack of exhibiting venues in New Zealand in the 1950s, has doubtless contributed to the relatively low profile this artist has been accorded in New Zealand art history.

PLATE 18

Jean Horsley was born in 1913 and studied at Elam and Chelsea Schools of Art. She exhibited at the Auckland Society of Arts from 1935–40, and studied under Colin McCahon. In 1946–47 she travelled to Japan and in 1948–49 to South Africa in conjunction with her job as a physiotherapist. From 1960–68 she lived and painted in London, assimilating all she could of contemporary art there. She exhibited at the Commonwealth Institute in 1961, at the Whitechapel Gallery, and in 1966 had a solo exhibition at the Drian Galleries. Throughout this period she also sent work back to New Zealand for exhibition and came in contact with other expatriate artists Ralph Hotere, Bill Culbert and Ted Bullmore.

In 1968 she emigrated to America, working again as a physiotherapist, and was able to satisfy at first hand her great enthusiasm for abstract expressionism in the work of artists such as de Kooning, Motherwell and Guston. Little painting was completed over this period of working in New York, economic survival being the predominant concern, but since the artist's return to New Zealand she has been painting consistently and has had one-woman exhibitions in 1984 and 1985. The beginning of this year (March 1986) has seen her topical *Halley's Comet* series exhibited at DKD café in Auckland.

Jean Horsley's work from the early sixties, when she moved into her version of abstract expressionism, was probably among some of the more adventurous and avant-garde work being produced by New Zealand artists of that period. Examples include 'Mark O', 1960, (Auckland City Art Gallery); 'Time Past' and 'Dancing Figures' both 1962 (the artist). 'Dancing Figures' displays

the characteristically gestural brushwork of the abstract expressionists combined with Horsley's interest in calligraphy retained from her earlier visits to Japan and still evident in some of her most recent works like 'Magic Writing', 1985 (private collection, Auckland).

PLATE 19

Alexis Hunter was born in Auckland in 1948, studied at Elam School of Fine Arts, Auckland University, and moved to London in 1972, where she has continued to live and work. She became involved in feminist groups in the early seventies and curated the opening exhibition at the Women's Free Alliance Gallery in 1976. From that year Hunter worked on a series of photographic narrative images, exhibiting feminist and other subjects involving social comment at a number of shows including the Hayward Annual 1977, and in 1978 at the Institute of Contemporary Arts. 'Approaches to Fear', shown at the Institute of Contemporary Arts, as with other works from this phase, explored and challenged the construct of femininity in Western culture. 'The Marxist's Wife (still does the housework)', 1978 (Edward Totah Gallery, London) is a well-known work which comments satirically and pointedly on a major lack in Marxist philosophy and practice. With works such as these Hunter's reputation as a major and feminist artist in Britain became secure. This was further reinforced in 1982 when she was chosen as a British representative at the Sydney Biennale.

Hunter also exhibits her work in Europe and America, has written on feminism and the arts and for part of 1986 was employed on a temporary visiting lectureship at the University of Houston, Texas. She continues to exhibit regularly in New Zealand.

In 1982 she returned to painting, developing a version of neo-expressionism. This change roughly coincided with her series of works relating to Greek and Christian mythology (the *Male Myths* series) where she engaged in a conscious re-visioning, a 'looking at historical myths as gender propaganda'. More recent work has explored animal/monster imagery to express meanings of sexual and socio-political significance.

'Rivers of the Moon' was painted by Hunter for an exhibition at Auckland's New Vision Gallery in 1985. This dramatic work with its fluid gestural and very red paintwork centres on the disturbing image of woman with monster sprouting from her head. (Memories of the miraculous births of Greek mythology?) To Hunter, the work signifies an aspect of women's experience of menstruation — this is also indicated by the title — and the mask, revealing rather than concealing eyes and face, refers perhaps to that periodic engagement with a different layer or sense of self. The monster, likewise, may express that cyclic release of energy with its potential for creative expression.

PLATE 20

Megan Jenkinson was born in 1958 in Hamilton, studied at Elam School of Fine Arts, Auckland University

1976–79 and gained her Bachelor of Arts in Photography in 1980. She has worked as a photographic technician and is currently a lecturer in Photography at Elam. Her first major one-woman show was *Discovering Galapagos* at Real Pictures Gallery, Auckland in 1982. Since then she has had work exhibited in other solo and group exhibitions, including the 1984 Polaroid Exhibition at Photokina, Cologne and at the Photographers' Gallery London. In 1984 Megan Jenkinson was awarded a Queen Elizabeth II Arts Council grant to attend workshops in the USA and at Mois de la Photographie in Paris.

As an artist working in the medium of photography, Jenkinson is concerned with technical change and advancement, and, in her words, 'with working on developing its potential creatively'. She has explored a number of techniques including hand-colouring, colour xerox and cyanotype and concentrates on work in colour often employing collage. While aesthetically exquisite and often making subtle use of *trompe d'oeil* devices, many of Jenkinson's works operate on additional levels: 'Creation and Modern Western Illusion of Power' comments on notions of might and alternative values of receptivity; in 'Flora', a self-portrait, the image cleverly side-steps an (anticipated) conventional femininity by Jenkinson's adoption of an assertively direct expression.

In 'Domestic Heartache I', Jenkinson uses soft beige-pinks and browns with the monochrome of the Braque reproduction to provide a ground for her delicately scattered 'actual' and collaged fragments of broken pottery. The title wryly refers to the breakage and the image conveys a further emotional dimension by reference to 'love' in the detail of the little red heart. Even the sound of the name Braque (Jenkinson suggests) may further underscore the meaning.

PLATE 21

Robyn Kahukiwa was born in Sydney of New Zealand parents. Her tribe is Ngati Porou and she is also affiliated to Te Arawa by marriage. She has three children and lives at Titahi Bay near Wellington. With no formal art training, Robyn Kahukiwa began painting in the late sixties when her children were young. She stresses that she has always painted from her taha Maori base: 'This part of me,' she says, 'is the inspiration of my work and my work is growing with the knowledge of my Maori side.' She adds that 'about five years ago I also began to look consciously at where I was going as a woman and how my work is definitely conceived with acknowledgement of my femaleness . . .'

Her sense of being Maori and her commitment to feminism were two strands which became integrated in her major one-woman exhibition *Wahine Toa* which toured Aotearoa in 1983. In this important series of paintings, drawings and prints, Kahukiwa focused on reclaiming the women of Maori mythology, with retelling myths which (like Alexis Hunter in her *Male Myths* series) she felt had been told for too long from a male perspective. The powerfully iconic 'Hinetitama' (Dawn

'maid' and mother of humankind) is the best-known image from the series and it also appears on the cover of the book based on the exhibition. The style of *Wahine Toa* combined a realist figurative style with elements of symbolism and other motifs from traditional Maori arts.

In 1982 Robyn Kahukiwa received a grant from the Maori and South Pacific Arts Council to research and work on the *Wahine Toa* project; in 1983 she was joint prizewinner of the Montana Art Award and she has received two Maspac awards (in 1981 and 1985). She has received a Queen Elizabeth II Arts Council Award for 1986. The artist has also illustrated a number of children's books.

'He Toa Takitahi', along with other recent painting by Kahukiwa, marks a shift in style to a freer, more expressive use of paint. As the proverb text printed opposite the image indicates, it points to the significance to contemporary Maori of a sense of ancestral connectiveness and to a sense of strength in the contemporary Maori community. This large and imposing painting is a part of an exhibition *Te Ao Marama: Seven Maori Artists*, which was displayed at the Sydney Opera House and is due to tour other Australian centres later in 1986.

PLATE 22

Emily Karaka, born 1952 (Waikato, Ngati Maniapoto, Nga Puhi).

I have always drawn from my inner world to communicate, tell, feel — pass on. My first oil painting (Form 2), was to be a study of a red rose in a vase — I produced a turbulent black bull. I remember painting tangi scenes, old kuia with writhing twisted knuckles and anguished pained faces, and aunties hid these.

I had a dream, spiritually/physically felt hapu (had my three children by then) gave birth to me — the Maori painter.

In this dream, my first in full colour, I approached a green island, chased by two psyche, before me kohatu — as I was to be devoured. I penetrated and became one with this table/altar, rock slab — ecstatic orgasmic union tangata whenua — of the land.

This dream happened when I had my first show, I sat under the tree near my old jail cell studio at Outreach and wept, as everyone acclaimed.

Although I now have my own work area, I still feel I'm in a jail cell — communicating. As a Maori woman, mother, liberationist, rape victim, I have much to say, and now nurtured by and enforced by my people, the tangata whenua of Aotearoa — I will bring into the chamber/vaults of reflection, the mirrored stories of the costs, changes, growth, life and death of our society.

Ka tangi te titi — The cry of the titi
Ka tangi te kaka — The cry of the kaka
Ka tangi ahau ki ahau — The cry of me in me
Tihei Mauri ora! — The sneeze of Maori life!

On my work
The landscape, BLACK
The bones, bared, WHITE
The dance, rained, blood RED . . .

Art is a word, you gave me LIFE
ART is an end, in ITSELF
Karanga mate, Karanga mate, Karanga mate.

Portrait of Dad becomes a tree
and the land march crosses the bridge
Portrait of Mavis and Joannie Hawke never completed
Cut off, arrested for trespass
Mother and child pierced on a cross
'Confiscated' . . . in Aotea Square

ART against trespass
Paintings opening up — A CHALLENGE
Empty kai sacks
A 'SUNRISE' industry . . . I'm told.

PLATE 23

Doris Lusk was born in Dunedin in 1916, and studied at
Dunedin School of Art with Charlton Edgar, R.N. Field,
Gordon Tovey and Russell Clark among her tutors and
Anne Hamblett and Colin McCahon among her fellow
students. She taught art for three years, engaged in some
commercial art work, then married and moved to
Christchurch in 1941. In 1947 she tutored in pottery at
Opawa and from 1967 to 1981 was employed as a lecturer
at Canterbury University School of Art. She continues
to live and work in Christchurch.

Doris Lusk exhibited regularly with The Group in
Christchurch until the last show in 1977, at the
Canterbury Society of Arts, and in many other New
Zealand centres. She has had two retrospectives (1965 and
1972), was awarded the Hay's prize for watercolour in
1966 and the National Bank award in 1968.

The artist has worked consistently from the early
forties, producing a large amount of work, mostly
concentrating on landscape painting. Well-known works
such as 'Tobacco Fields, Pangatotara' (1943, Auckland
City Art Gallery) and 'Tobacco Fields, Nelson' (1941,
Hocken Library, Dunedin), like the best of other works
by Lusk of that time and into the fifties, display
connections with a late cubist style and a concern with
simplifying and solidifying landscape forms. These have
some similarities to contemporary work of other region-
alists such as Rita Angus and Colin McCahon. 'The
Pumping Station', 1958 (illustrated in Pound, Plate 21)
shows a later development of this approach. Some of her
more recent work, however, has been involved in more
urban imagery and her fine series of *Arcade Awnings*,
1976 (Auckland City Art Gallery) were painted in the
Italian cities of Bologna and Venice. In other recent works
Doris Lusk demonstrates her continuing search for a
personal style in landscape painting.

The early 'Canterbury Plains from the Cashmere Hills'
is a landscape devoid of buildings and overt signs of
human activity. Effectively horizontal in format to
enhance the sense of sweep and distance, it interestingly
focuses on the hollow of the fertile green valley in the
centre of the picture space, with this and the distant
shoulders of hills foregrounded by a fringe of exotic pines.

PLATE 24

Vivian Lynn was born in Wellington and studied at
Canterbury University School of Art. She married in
1956, had two children, and her first solo exhibition was
in 1966. Since then she has exhibited regularly in group
and one-woman exhibitions and has undertaken a
number of study tours: to Australia in 1964 and 1983;
to the USA in 1972, where she furthered her interest in
print-making and began to develop an interest in three-
dimensional work; and to Europe and to the USA again
in 1981. Vivian Lynn has been an active supporter of the
Women's Art Movement in New Zealand and from
1983–84 was involved in setting up the Women's Art
Archive. She lives with the artist Jurgen Waibel.

From 1973–80 Vivian Lynn's involvement in silk-screen
printing resulted in the complex *Book of Forty Images*
and the *Playground* print series. During this period she
also began to work on environmental pieces including the
five-year project of 'Taupata-ma': an environmental
sculpture at her home whose basic layout is related to
the structure of the leaf of the indigenous taupata-ma tree.
This, together with an extension of the idea into landscape
architecture, the *Colombo St Urban Plan* concept, were
expressions of her concern with ecological and social
issues, environmental aesthetics and her belief that
'gardens have, since earliest times, been animated by the
female principle'.

Vivian Lynn's ability to work on projects where
meaning is multilayered and where the scale is often large
is evidenced in much of her more recent work: as a New
Zealand representative at *ANZART*-in-Hobart in 1983;
in her 'Lamella-Lamina' piece, the G^u*arden Gates* series
of 1982 and most recently, her installation 'The Gates of
the Goddess — a Southern Crossing attended by the
Goddess' at the Govett-Brewster Art Gallery, New
Plymouth. This work consists of three massive panels,
two making a passage structure and the third the focal
point with the Goddess image at the end. It is a work
which ties together various major concerns of Lynn's: an
interest in installation work; her sense of connectiveness
with Oceanic culture (in her use of bark cloth as the main
material); with her interest in matriarchal cultures and
a concern to represent previously taboo aspects of
women's biological experience in the references to
menstruation (the 'pocket' shapes on the left-hand panel)
and to menocease.

PLATE 25

Molly Macalister was born in 1920 in Invercargill and
studied at Canterbury University College of Art under
Francis Shurrock. She moved to Auckland in 1943 and
married in 1945. In 1959 she took part in a group show
at the Auckland City Art Gallery with sculptors Ann

Severs and Alison Duff and she continued work until her death in 1979. She has one son.

Public commissions by Molly Macalister include the well-known, monumental 'Maori Chief' (1964–66) for Auckland City Council; the friendly 'Little Bull' (1967) at Hamilton; the 'Ark' for the Jewish Synagogue, Auckland, and during the seventies work for the State Insurance Building and the North Shore Crematorium, both in Auckland. Macalister also illustrated a number of children's books and completed some murals for the Wilson Home for Crippled Children.

Like the careers of some other artists of her generation, Molly Macalister's was somewhat limited by conditions in New Zealand in the post-war years of the fifties. Being a woman artist in those years had its added difficulties and being a woman sculptor was even more isolating and unusual. Not only were social attitudes rather rigid, but there was also the problem of the lack of dealer galleries for exhibiting work and the lack of facilities for bronze casting. These problems were partly addressed by Macalister: she, Alison Duff and Ann Severs organised drawing sessions together, for example, and Macalister began to experiment with alternative materials, notably reinforced concrete. Her subjects ranged from animal studies to figure studies and heads ('Head', 1941–42, a wedding present for her husband, is a powerful example) to more abstract works in the seventies. Stylistically Oceanic art was of great importance to her as was contemporary sculpture, particularly the work of Henry Moore which she saw at the 1956 exhibition at the Auckland City Art Gallery. In some later works it is possible to see something of the effects of her involvement in Zen Buddhism.

'Cat' is one delightful example of Macalister's several cat sculptures. It is beautifully and amusingly simplified in form and can be viewed equally satisfyingly from many different angles. The artist gave this work to art historian Marcus Sopher and his wife Joan, resident in Berkeley, California. It was included in the 1982 Memorial exhibition of Macalister's work at the Auckland City Art Gallery and is now in the collection of George Haydn and family.

PLATE 26

Ruhia Oketopa was born as Ruhia Reihana in 1914 at Ohaki village in Taupo. Her father is Tuwharetoa while her mother is Te Arawa of Rotorua. She married and lived in Taupo where she reared her family and spent most of her married life. She now lives in Te Ngae, Rotorua.

Ruhia's background in the crafts of raranga and whatu comes from the Taupo area where a great deal of weaving and plaiting was still done in Maori communities throughout the surrounding districts during and following World War I. As a young girl Ruhia took a casual interest in the plaiting work done by the womenfolk of her village. It was commonplace for her and her peers to assist the older women in gathering and preparing material for plaiting kits and mats for everyday use. On such occasions the young women would observe their superiors at work, although no actual teaching of novices took place. Learning took the form of watching, followed by random weaving of plaiters' work when they left their work for short periods. This is how Ruhia developed the techniques which enabled her to produce her ceremonial whariki, which are kept for very special occasions and functions such as the lying-in-state of persons of standing in the local or greater Maori community. Ruhia is still actively involved in the art of raranga and is currently plaiting a mat for presentation to a group in Wellington.

PLATE 27

Maria Olsen was born in 1945 in Christchurch and studied at Canterbury University School of Art, graduating in 1964. She completed a post-graduate Diploma in teaching in 1965, worked as a screen-printer from 1966–67, then moved to Australia where she taught art for a year, returning to New Zealand in 1969. In 1971 in New Plymouth she made screen-printed fabrics and from 1974 has lived in Auckland with her husband, artist John Parry, and their three daughters. She started exhibiting her work regularly from the mid seventies and had her first solo show in 1980. In 1984 Maria Olsen was an *ANZART* representative at the Edinburgh Festival and in 1985 a New Zealand representative at *Perspecta*, Sydney. She has travelled in America and France and has made a number of visits to India. Historical artists she has admired include Goya and Velasquez, while Cucchi and Kiefer are two contemporary artists whose work she particularly respects.

Working within the general framework of the new figuration and in a neo-expressionist related style, Olsen's work continues to range from drawing to painting, to sculpture. Her earlier works often incorporated domestic references, using a delicate and light tonal range and showing a concern with spatial ambiguities. Working on a P.E.P. scheme at Auckland Hospital in 1982 she experimented with larger scale work using egg-tempera and pastel, a development which was crucial to her subsequent work. Recent work has developed certain motifs from the earlier phase, notably the bones, which have evolved in various ways, either as sculptural objects in themselves or imaged in paintings and pastels. In these works an increasingly expressive technique has been used together with a richer, darker and more sombre colour range. A recent exhibition which included the work 'Embrace' (Chartwell Collection, Centre for Contemporary Art, Hamilton) displayed large painted sculptural pieces with a monumental presence, paintings, and paintings which employed sculptural elements. It included a number of works which continued Olsen's exploration of a recently evolved motif, the vessel or cauldron (see her 'On Remembering Water', 1985, Chartwell Collection, Plate 28 in Pound). 'Embrace' is a powerfully evocative work which is unusual in her work in its more direct human reference.

PLATE 28

Glenda Randerson was born in 1949 in Otorohanga, studied at Elam School of Fine Arts, Auckland University under Colin McCahon and Garth Tapper, and graduated in 1970. She has two children, is married and lives in Auckland. Glenda Randerson has exhibited since 1970 in a number of group and one-woman shows, mainly in Wellington and Auckland. The meticulous detail of her realist style means, of necessity, that solo shows occur only once every few years. In 1984 she won the Team McMillan Ford Award Competition for her 'Brunch, Freeman's Bay'.

Randerson is an admirer of the work of artists like Giorgio Morandi and Mary Cassatt and, within the New Zealand context, the work and the dedication of Rita Angus have provided her with inspiration and a strong role model. Much of Randerson's work of the seventies has focused on realist interpretations of bourgeois interiors and still life arrangements, where carefully chosen scenes and objects were painted in subtle tones and bathed in a cool light. 'Persimmons', 1979 (Auckland City Art Gallery) is an example. Its motif of the view to the outside world framed by the window is also a frequent device in her work.

Recent works have extended the range of her subject matter to figure subjects including portraits, usually of friends, such as fellow artists Carole Shepheard ('Portrait of Carole Shepheard', 1982, Bank of New Zealand collection) and Rodney Fumpston ('Rodney Fumpston', 1986, the artist). She has also recently worked on studies of nude figures in interiors.

'Doll's Head with Matisse Painting' is a small work which sees Randerson effectively extending her tonal range and her selection of objects: the painting is characterised by a warmer colouring and greater diversity of paint texture, and the objects themselves and their interrelationships suggest a wealth of associations and ideas, among them inspiration and growth.

PLATE 29

Puti Hineaupounamu Rare was born in 1916 at the village of Oparure in Te Kuiti. She is of the Ngati Maniapoto tribe. Her mother, Tira Hinewai Tumohe, grew up in an environment where the traditional crafts of raranga and whatu played a significant role in the community. It was accepted that Puti would inherit her mother's skills and in turn Tira Tumohe ensured that she handed on all that she knew to her daughter. Puti served her apprenticeship well, and continues to weave splendid garments or plait highly decorative kete in her urban home in Auckland.

The very finely woven taniko items are samples made by both Puti and her mother. The work with the turned-up edge is a fine piece made by Puti at the age of fourteen years. It is made of fibre extracted from the flax blade in its green state, and usage has tended to dull its colouring. The different colours come from certain native trees and shrubs as well as black mud. The larger taniko piece has a brilliance lacking in the smaller sample, as it has had little use and exposure to sunlight. It is the work of Tira Tumohe.

Named patterns were used in the decorative panels and bands were selected to edge the hemlines and front edges of the cloaks. Nihoniho, mawhiwhiti, and aranui are some of the names of such patterns. Their use enhanced the fine work in the body of the patterns.

PLATE 30

Pauline Rhodes was born in Christchurch in 1937, studied art at Wellington Polytech in 1960, and from 1961–64 lived at Westport. In 1964 she left New Zealand and lived in Nigeria, working on terracotta sculpture, pottery and also on bronze casting with a traditional bronze caster. The whole experience of Nigerian life and culture she feels has had a lasting influence. Later she toured Europe and lived in England from 1967, continuing her work in sculpture, visiting quarries and seeing major art exhibitions including the Picasso, Moore, Hepworth and Caro. In 1970 she returned to New Zealand and settled in Christchurch where she studied at Canterbury University School of Fine Arts 1972–74 and began outdoor sculptural projects. Her first solo exhibition was at the Canterbury Society of Arts in 1977. She has exhibited regularly in New Zealand and participated in the 1979 Australian Sculpture Triennial in Melbourne and the 1980 Sydney Biennale. Pauline Rhodes is married with two sons and is a long distance runner.

While Rhodes has worked on a number of gallery installations, her ongoing outdoor projects (over the last seven years) which she calls *Extensums* are more important to her. She states that 'the point about my work is that it is a continuum of ephemeral projects developed over a period of many years, mostly in isolation . . .' She continues to stress that 'the very nature of the work makes records difficult and always inadequate — the work is to be caught on the wing, experienced in the now'.

'Intensums '85' (installed in the Auckland City Art Gallery) comprised two related entities, one closed, the other open. Like other works by Rhodes it can be interpreted on one level as a kind of metaphor for the cyclic processes of natural systems, involving as it does notions of 'groundedness', growth, transformation, change and decay. In a statement accompanying the installation, Rhodes wrote that she likes 'to be doing work which is self-generating, which has its own continuum of energy, and which evokes universal life forces'. Her statement ends with a quotation from Beckett: 'I would like to *leave a stain upon the silence.*'

PLATE 31

Helen Flora Scales was born in 1888 in Wellington of parents who were both 'Sunday' painters. As a child growing up in the Eastern Hutt hills, she drew and painted animals and was encouraged by her father to enrol at the Frank Calderon School of Animal Painting, London, where she lived from 1908–12. Back in New Zealand she worked as a V.A.D. during the war years, managing to continue painting and exhibiting her work. From 1921 until her father's death in 1928 she had various jobs including employment as housemaid and canning factory worker near Nelson. After that she lived frugally on a small annuity left by her father, and left for France, where she studied for a time at the Grande Chaumière, Paris. In the early 1930s she met Frances Hodgkins and Gwen Knight in the south of France and on Gwen Knight's advice went to Munich in 1931 to attend the Hans Hoffmann School — an experience crucial to her subsequent work.

In 1934 Flora Scales returned to New Zealand to care for her mother and it was at this time that she had five meetings with Toss Woollaston who studied her notebooks from the Hoffmann School — crucial to *his* subsequent work, as he freely acknowledges. 'She taught me how to think . . .' he said in an interview in 1984, (*New Zealand Herald*, 15 June). The painting 'Mediterranean Village' (1938, Dowse Art Gallery, Lower Hutt) shows the late-cubist style which together with the Mediterranean colouring was characteristic of her work during this period. In the New Zealand context it looked extraordinary to reviewers: her work (according to researcher Barbi de Lange, a source for much of this information on Scales) was dubbed typical of 'the earthquake school'.

During the Second World War Flora Scales was interned in France for two years and much of her work, which had been in storage, was destroyed. Little is currently known about her life during the fifties and sixties, except that she continued to live and work in France and England. She returned to New Zealand in 1972, and exhibited in the 1975 *New Zealand's Women Painters* exhibition at Auckland City Art Gallery, curated by Anne Kirker and Eric Young. In 1976 a solo exhibition of her painting was held at the same gallery. Gretchen Albrecht's response to the works was 'immediate and intense' and as a result of Albrecht's contacting her, the two artists maintained a relationship up until Flora Scales's death in 1985 at ninety-eight.

The charming 'Suburbs outside Paris' like most of the artist's work is small in scale. It displays her characteristically broad yet delicate handling of paint, her distinctive colouring and her interest in synthesising the various spatial depths of field so that the image works coherently on the picture plane.

PLATE 32

Carole Shepheard was born in Taumarunui in 1945 and studied at Elam School of Fine Arts, Auckland University from 1964 to 1967. Since then she has held a number of teaching positions, has led several workshops in the arts and has curated exhibitions such as the Outreach *Women in the Arts*, 1980, and (with Christine Hellyar) the 1985 *ANZART 'Artists' Books'* exhibition at Auckland City Art Gallery. Carole Shepheard was a Visiting Printmaker at the Crippled Children's Society in Auckland in 1985 and she has been involved in collaborative feminist art

projects such as *Lifescape* in 1982 (facilitated by Juliet Batten) and *Sybil's Leaves* (organiser Faith Wilding) at the Museum of Modern Art, Los Angeles, also 1982. That year Shepheard was awarded a Queen Elizabeth II Arts Council grant for travel and study in America. She is married, has two children and lives in Auckland.

In the earlier seventies while her children were very young, Shepheard stitched and crocheted, batiked and patchworked clothes for her small boutique; it was not until 1976, when the children were older, that she consciously re-entered the 'fine' arts arena and embarked on an etching course. Since 1977 she has exhibited regularly in both group and one-woman shows. In common with some contemporary American women artists her feminist work has incorporated women's traditional art skills, challenged assumptions on the arts/crafts dichotomy, and imaginatively extended conventional boundaries of 'craft' work.

Shepheard's more recent work has continued her involvement with the grid motif, combining this with areas of freer paint application, as in the large circular 'Amazon Shield II' (1984, private collection, Wellington). 'John', shown at the Outreach *Images of Men* exhibition, 1981, is a large modular piece made of individually boxed images. This multi-faceted portrait includes images of 'John's face, various parts of his body and shows the subject in various roles — for instance as father and also as musician. By doing this, the work both challenges traditional notions of the portrait and also begins to develop an alternative convention to the stubborn tradition of the erotic (and usually depersonalised) female nude. Shepheard depicts the erotic *male* nude — individualised.

PLATE 33

May Smith was born in Simla, India in 1906. She was encouraged to take up painting when confined to bed for long periods as the result of a hip operation. Peter Shaw (*Art New Zealand* 28: 46–51, and a source for much of the following information) reports her describing the importance of her experience in India for her subsequent work, particularly the visual experience of being '. . . surrounded by oriental buildings, fabrics and hand-wrought objects'. Certainly rich colouring and a strong feeling for decorative design and actual work with fabric are very much part of her later career as an artist, although she initially specialised in engraving at Elam School of Fine Arts where she studied from 1924–28 (after coming to New Zealand in 1921). Encouraged by A.J. Fisher she continued her studies at the Royal College of Art, London, graduating in 1931. During the thirties she embarked on some fabric designing and printing and took up painting seriously while absorbing the art of the French School, then much exhibited in London. She was also involved in socialism and in activities connected with the Spanish Civil War. She went to Spain in 1933, where she met Frances Hodgkins — the first of a number of contacts with the older expatriate artist. Back in New Zealand in

1939 May Smith continued painting and fabric designing and printing, producing work that in the context of New Zealand painting at the time was highly innovative: from this period come her well-known 'Characterisation in Colour' (1941, Auckland City Art Gallery and Plate 33 in Pound) 'Canal, Camden Town' (present whereabouts unknown) and the luscious 'Pumpkins' (1941, private collection, Auckland). These three works show her penchant for bold, simplified and semi-abstract design, and richly decorative colour. The later years of her marriage (1944–52) were not productive artistically, and from then until 1967 she was employed as art teacher at Epsom Girls' Grammar School, Auckland. In 1967 she settled in Coromandel and has continued to paint there since her remarriage in 1974.

'Animal Kingdom' was printed soon after her return to New Zealand from Europe. It displays her graphic abilities well but it is also a particularly interesting image in terms of its content which reads as a kind of allegory on the theme of war and nature and is almost certainly a response to war-torn Europe of the forties. In the centre of the image helmeted soldiers aim at each other and two male figures fight; to the left a mother and child and others flee from the scene of battle, this island of conflict and destruction surrounded by the innocent and peaceable representatives of the 'animal kingdom'.

PLATE 34

Marté Szirmay was born in Budapest in 1946, migrated to New Zealand in 1957 and studied at Elam School of Fine Arts, Auckland University from 1965 to 1968. She has received a number of awards, was Frances Hodgkins Fellow in 1971 and 1972, and in 1984 was Visiting Professor of Sculpture at Governor State University of Chicago. Marté Szirmay has exhibited regularly in New Zealand from 1968 and has participated in the Mildura Triennials of 1970 and 1973, Arteder '82 at Bilboa, Spain, the New Zealand Craft Council *Kahurangi* in Los Angeles 1984 and in Tokyo 1985. She has completed a number of public commissions in New Zealand and one in Singapore (New Zealand Foreign Affairs, 1984). Her public works in New Zealand include the well-known 'Smirnoff' sculpture in Newmarket, Auckland, 1969; the 1975–76 Otago Medical School work; the 1979 sculpture for the New Zealand Housing Corporation Building, Manukau City Centre; and the Marac House sculpture for the New Zealand Peace Foundation, also at Manukau city, in 1984.

Marté Szirmay has a long-standing interest in prehistoric art, having studied anthropology at Auckland University, taken part in archaeological digs and visited many sites both in New Zealand and in other countries. At Elam Szirmay valued the example of dedicated artists such as Colin McCahon and later, while travelling in England, the experience of meeting Barbara Hepworth was important. Artists of interest to her have included Mantegna, Piero della Francesca, Brancusi, Hepworth and Caro. Szirmay has worked as a teacher and over the

last two years has been involved in the Outreach 'open studio' programme. Until recently the bulk of her work has been primarily abstract. She has used cast and sheet metal, cast resin, cast paper and bronze.

'Sculpture for the Gibbs' Garden' was a private commission, the requirements simply a work that related to its setting. The sculpture admirably fulfils its brief: set across from a patio space, it provides an interesting focus for the garden-side living areas of the house (designed by Manning Mitchell, Architects, completed in 1984) and its reflective surface picks up colours from the architecture, the ground cover and the sky. The disc shape also cleverly relates to the circular cutout in the metal roof, so that it seems, as the artist says 'as if it was the hole that fell out'.

PLATE 35

Diggeress Rangituatahi Te Kanawa (née Hetet) of Te Kuiti has throughout her life been active in promoting the arts of raranga and weaving. She was born in 1920 of Ngati Maniapoto descent and by following in her mother Rangimarie Hetet's footsteps soon became proficient and skilled. Like Ruhia Oketopa (Plate 26) she was never actually taught the art, but rather watched and observed, participating randomly whenever the opportunity arose. In this way she learnt how to prepare and make feather cloaks, mats, kete and piupiu. The decorative band at the top of her piupiu (Plate 35) is an example of taniko weaving, while the stepped pattern incorporated in the skirt is known as the poutama. Native trees and shrubs such as the kowhai were used for the colour in the taniko, while the black colour was achieved by placing the muka in black mud. The proportions of this skirt indicates it is for the use of women when performing poi and other dances. The way the piupiu is structured allows for lively and free movement of the flax strands to complement the body movement in dance.

As with many of her peers Diggeress is committed to perpetuating traditional Maori arts. She is continually called upon to attend conferences to demonstrate and teach raranga and weaving to women of all ages. She is encouraged by the enthusiasm of young and old in pursuing what is for her a cultural treasure.

PLATE 36

Pauline Thompson was born in Auckland in 1942 and studied at Elam School of Fine Arts in 1960 and from 1963–64. She exhibited regularly from the mid-sixties to early seventies and after a break of several years (in common with a number of other women artists with families) returned to working and exhibiting regularly again in 1980. She was awarded a Queen Elizabeth II Arts Council grant in 1984 and continues to live and work in Auckland. She has three children. She has been a pupil of Sufi teacher Abdullah Dougan.

Her recent paintings tend to be executed in series; some of the subjects she has explored include Auckland and Wellington city views, Norfolk Island scenes, the Bounty mutiny and, most recently, episodes from the life of Mother Aubert, New Zealand's nineteenth century humanitarian and saint-like nun who cared for social outcasts, the poor and the underprivileged. Thompson's very individual work can be seen in the general context of the romantic strand of neo-expressionism; she uses an expressive realist style and a lyrical colour range centring on pinks, oranges, mauves and blues. Her city views, for instance 'Auckland View: Central Police Station, Guy Fawkes Night' (1982, Auckland City Art Gallery) focus on well-known landmarks with a vision that, by simplifying and altering, eerily transforms the familiar.

Thompson has also explored the very difficult territory of imaging intellectually and physically handicapped children: a recent very moving work effectively appropriates part of Manet's 'Olympia' (and clothes her) and adds the image of a tiny hydrocephalic baby. Thompson is an admirer of Manet's work, also Goya, Velasquez and Turner and, among contemporary artists, McCahon and Morley.

'Burning of the Bounty with Tahitian and English Figures' belongs, appropriately enough, to the New Zealand film-maker Roger Donaldson, who directed the recent *Bounty* film. It is one of the paintings in Thompson's recreation of this South Seas saga which includes larger-scale figures, and in doing so can be seen to mark the transition to her current involvement with figure subjects. Interestingly, Pauline Thompson herself is a descendant of a Bounty mutineer.

PLATE 37

Teuane Tibbo was born in Apia, Samoa in 1893 near Robert Louis Stevenson's estate Vailima. She recalled a request from him for a lock of her hair for a watch-chain, which — frightened by her first sight of a *Palagi* — she initially refused. She spent her childhood in Pago Pago, married, later remarrying and returning to Western Samoa where she and her husband were involved in early independence struggles. They came to New Zealand at the end of World War II.

She began painting at the age of seventy-one as the direct result of two visionary dreams immediately preceding the experience of seeing original paintings for the first time — her daughter's. She described her second dream: 'I was standing out in the night. My hair was long and black . . . the sky was blue and full of stars . . . all the stars started falling down all around me and when they fell down they were coming up big, big, like soap . . . like bubbles . . . I was queen of the stars . . . then I woke up. I told my husband and he said "I told you to go for a holiday!" '

Teuane Tibbo painted continuously from that time (1963) into the seventies, until her health became too poor. She died in 1984 at a rest home in Auckland. Self-taught as an artist and free of learned conventions, Teuane Tibbo painted with that brilliant child-like freshness of vision usually described as 'primitive' or 'naive' or more recently as typical of 'outsider art'. Her

colourful works, often with symmetrial compositions and bold decorative motifs, are joyful celebrations of her memories — and her imaginative reconstructions — of her early life in Samoa. Her range of subjects included fishing scenes, vases of brightly coloured flowers, firewalkers, *taro* gathering, *tapa* making, and scenes of community festivity (for example, 'The Wedding', private collection, Auckland). She was encouraged in her early efforts by Pat Hanly and was often given painting materials by Barry Lett Galleries, where she had a number of one-woman shows. Her works are in collections in New Zealand, Australia, Japan and Germany.

'Forceful' depicts a number of people engaged in various activities within a luxuriant tropical setting which the artist tilts boldly up to the picture plane for maximum decorative effect.

PLATE 38

Merylyn Tweedie was born in 1953 in Christchurch and studied at Canterbury University School of Fine Arts, graduating in 1975. She first exhibited her work that year, continuing into 1978, but with two small children did not return to regular exhibiting until 1983. Since 1983 she has had a number of one-woman exhibitions and has taken part in group shows including several organised by the Auckland Women Artists' Association, the *ANZART Artists' Books Show* of 1985, the *Still Life* exhibition at New Vision Gallery, Auckland and *The Word* at the Bishop Souter Art Gallery in Nelson. Merylyn Tweedie is a feminist and is involved in a number of womens' groups. She co-curated a photography exhibition for the Women Artists' Association *Photography as the Medium* at Outreach in 1985 and was a speaker at the Arts Council-organised Critics' Symposium at Wellington in February 1986. Tweedie is an admirer of the work of expatriate New Zealand artists Alexis Hunter and Boyd Webb. Her wide-ranging reading and interest in feminist theory is expressed both subtly and surprisingly in her often highly satirical works.

Much of Tweedie's work has focused on the human subject, her earlier images often of disturbingly blurred, almost Baconesque faces, where notions of identity, presence/absence and anxiety, were important. Recent works speak frequently of women's experience in a patriarchal society, incorporating found photographs, collage, hand-tinting and text in a very personal manner. These images and text, sometimes in a narrative sequence, attack sexist language ('Man the Cake Stall Girls! She'll be right! . . .') with wit. That together with her eye for curious images and odd conjunctions of image can produce most effectively challenging and thought-provoking work.

'the artist prepares' is a book work in which Tweedie employs her characteristic skill at choosing a curious image with a message that both baffles (the artist prepares . . . to hunt . . .) and challenges notions of who 'the artist' is. Just what she intends to saw down to size is left to the viewer's imagination.

PLATE 39

A. Lois White was born in Auckland in 1903, studied at Elam School of Fine Arts under A.J.C. Fisher and taught for eight years at Takapuna Grammar School, before becoming a tutor in painting at Elam until her retirement in 1963. She died in 1984.

She exhibited regularly from the thirties and into the fifties in group shows like the New Zealand Academy of Fine Arts exhibitions, when reviewers often singled out her work for praise, but it was not until after she was seventy (1973) that the first comprehensive one-woman exhibition of her work was held. She painted a number of murals, among them 'Magna Carta', for Southwell School, Hamilton, and 'Controversy', 1946, a commission from the W.E.A. which was unfortunately destroyed in the Elam fire of 1948. To a certain extent unfashionable in the sixties and seventies, and not concerned with the more mainstream tradition of landscape painting in New Zealand, her unique contribution to New Zealand art has received minimal attention in our major art history texts — and none for instance in Brown and Keith's *An Introduction to New Zealand Painting*. It is interesting to re-evaluate her work now, however, in the context of the current return to figuration in the arts — and a figuration which often includes social comment and myth and allegory, all also explored by White, as well as Biblical narrative and themes that were primarily decorative. Her general approach owed much to the influence and encouragement of A.J.C. ('Mr') Fisher, particularly his emphasis on drawing and construction, with design geared towards the expression of *ideas*, a notion important to White. Her commitment to socialism and her strong feelings about social injustice, are expressed for instance in 'The War Makers' (1937, Auckland City Art Gallery), one of her best-known works whose style also owes something to the influence of Stanley Spencer.

An interesting feature of her mythological and allegorical figure subjects is her frequent choice of those which involve or focus on women, for example: 'Persephone's return to Dementer', 'Dianne', 'Ode to Autumn', the personifications 'Winter' and 'Spring', 'Wind Witches', 'Trio' and 'Gay Ladies'.

'On the Air', like many of White's paintings, displays a complex collection of stylised figures rhythmically organised, each one representative of a particular walk of life and differing in her or his participation in or reaction to the scene.

PLATE 40

Robin White was born in Te Puke in 1946, studied at Epsom Girls' Grammar where she was encouraged in art by May Smith, and then at the School of Fine Arts, Auckland University from 1965 to 1967, where Colin McCahon was a particularly important influence. Her first one-woman exhibition was in 1970. She has worked full-time as an artist since 1972, after living at Bottle Creek, Paremata and moving to Otago Peninsula in 1971. In 1982 she and her husband and son moved to Tarawa, Kiribati. Robin White has exhibited frequently in New Zealand since the early seventies and continues to do so while resident in Kiribati. This year (1986) she is a New Zealand representative at the Sydney Biennale. She is part Pakeha and part Maori of Ngati Awa descent. She is a Baha'i.

The artist is well-known both as a painter and as a printmaker, but it is probably the wide currency of her screenprints that has made her particular version of regional realism familiar to a large public. These images of the New Zealand landscape, some with its provincial buildings, have a quality of clarity, simplification and concentration that has made them emblematic to many of a perceived 'essential' New Zealandness. Works like 'Mangaweka' (1973) for instance, have almost become secular icons of the rural scene. Robin White has acknowledged the significance to her of Rita Angus's work and her dedicated attitude to painting, describing this as an 'inspiration', and in White's painting and screenprint of her mother 'Florence at Harbour Cone' (1974 and 1975), she pays homage in the general positioning of the figure to Rita Angus's important portrait 'Betty Curnow' (1942, Auckland City Art Gallery). Recent work has developed in a new direction, exploring the medium of woodcut and responding in subject matter to the people, the environment and the language of Kiribati.

Although many have interpreted *A Buzzy Bee for Siulolovao* as a parody of fellow regionalist realist Don Binney's familiar iconography (as in Pound, Plate 4), the image has a more personal genesis: this Buzzy Bee, the artist explains, refers not only to the (uniquely New Zealand) toy given her by her Tongan friend Mere Meangata, mother of Siulolovao, when Robin was pregnant with her son Michael, but it also whimsically symbolises the arrival of the baby.

A glossary follows Plate 40.

Titles of paintings are opposite each plate. Note that the measurements give height before width.

Plate 1
ZENA ABBOTT
Scrolls
1980
canvas and sisal
2400mm x 2200mm x (depth) 1400mm
Fisher Gallery, Pakuranga

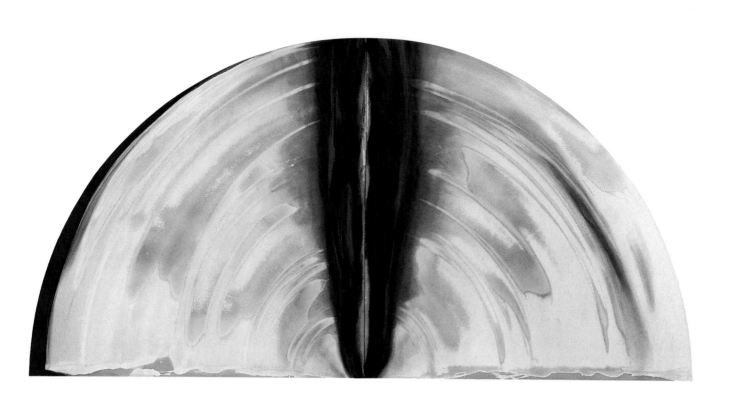

Plate 3
RITA ANGUS
Self-portrait
1936–37
oil on canvas
490mm x 390mm
Dunedin Public Art Gallery

Plate 4
INGRID BANWELL
An Indigenous Spring Specimen
1983
oil on customwood
540mm x 720mm
The artist

Plate 5
PHILIPPA BLAIR
Queen of Hearts
1985
flat-glass panel
561mm x 919mm
This work was made at Glassworks, Christchurch
by Suzanne Johnson and Ben Hanly.
The artist

Plate 6
KATE COOLAHAN
Filters
1974
oil paintings, windscreen, rope
1770mm (including rope at bottom) x 1230mm x (depth) 100mm
The artist

Plate 10
DI FFRENCH
The Useful Idiot and Arnolfini's Hat
1984
cibachrome photograph
543mm x 880mm

Plate 11
JACQUELINE FRASER
Kauri Installation, two details
Sue Crockford Gallery
1986
kauri planks, coloured twine, material remnants
1800mm x 390mm; 1800mm x 580mm
The artist

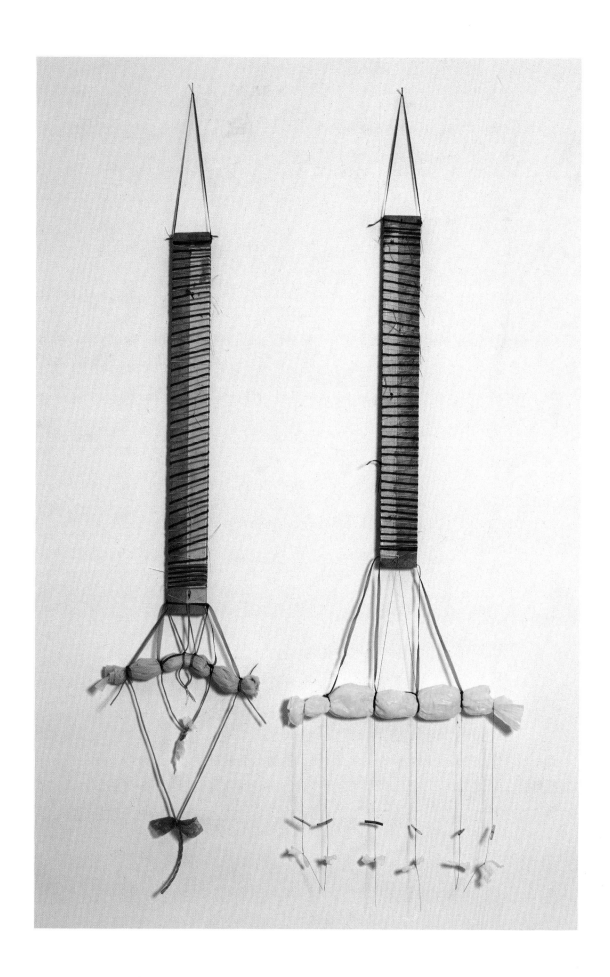

Plate 12
MATARENA GEORGE
Pansy Tivaevae
c. 1972
casement cotton and embroidery thread
2560mm x 2535mm
Matarena George Collection

Plate 13
CHRISTINE HELLYAR
Tool Trays (8 works from a set of 14)
1982
wood trays, fabric, stone, clay, feathers, fur felt,
natural fibres, brass nails
400mm x 400mm x 45mm (each tray)
Auckland City Art Gallery

Titles of *Tooltrays* (from top, left to right):
Birds of a feather flock; Skin scrapers; Tied bird stones on sticks;
Bird stones for brides; Bird stones pinned down for young brides;
Rocks for women's roads; Flax beaters; Rocks for women's roads.
Note: Trays rearranged for photography with the artist's permission.

The remaining six of the fourteen *Tool Trays* are titled:
Birds of a feather flock; Flax beaters; Moth rocks on roots;
Moth rocks not on sticks; Skin scrapers; Women's grubbers.

Plate 14
LOUISE HENDERSON
Still Life — Glass and Printed Cloth
c. 1950
oil on plate glass
360mm x 285mm
Private collection, Auckland

Plate 15
RANGIMARIE HETET (née Hursthouse)
He korowai
1970
he muka, he huru kiwi, he kereru
920mm x 1090mm
Rangimarie Hetet Collection, Te Kuiti

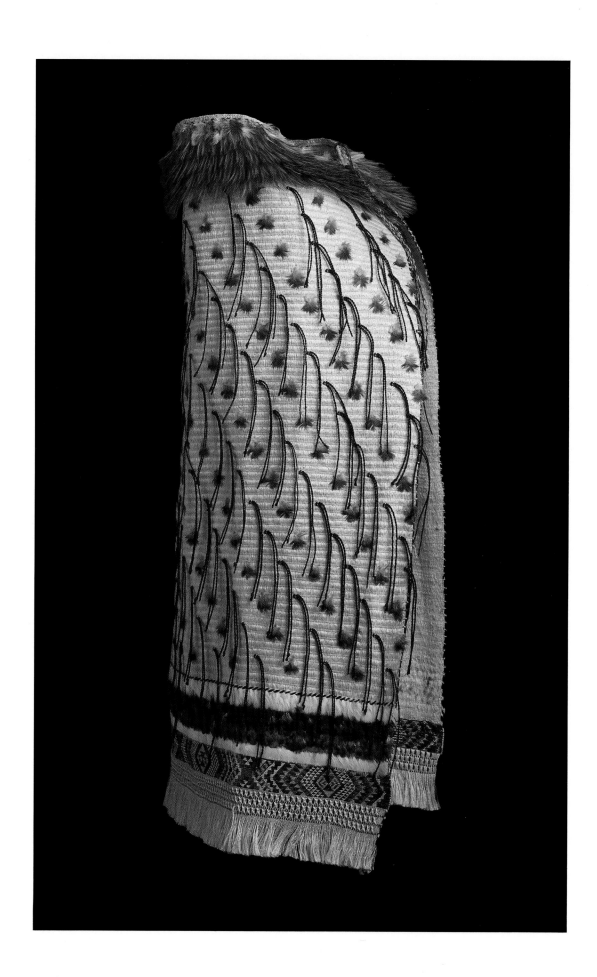

Plate 16
FRANCES HODGKINS
Zipp
1945
oil on canvas
632mm x 765mm
Robert McDougall Art Gallery, Christchurch

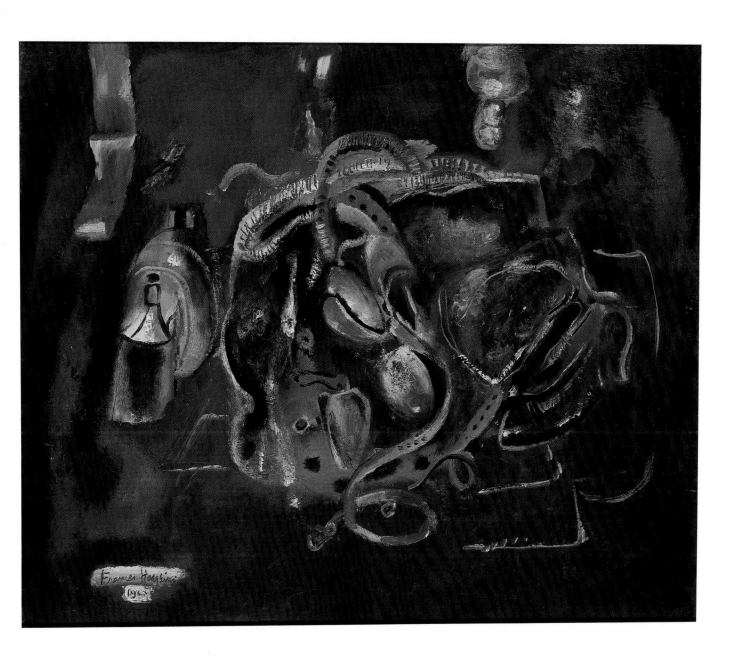

Plate 17
GABRIELLE HOPE
The Poet (Self-portrait)
1953
watercolour and gouache on paper
665mm x 495mm
Auckland City Art Gallery

GABRIELLE
1943.

Plate 18
JEAN HORSLEY
Dancing Figures
1962
oil on canvas
790mm x 1003mm
The artist

Plate 19
ALEXIS HUNTER
Rivers of the Moon
1985
oil on canvas
1818mm x 1214mm
Auckland City Art Gallery

Plate 20
MEGAN JENKINSON
Domestic Heartache I, with Poole in Pieces
1984
200mm x 541mm
polachrome
The artist

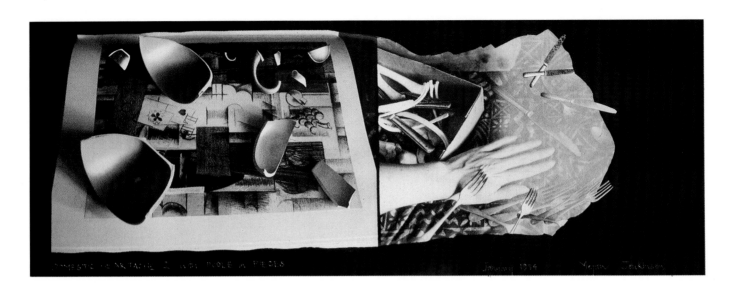

DOMESTIC MEMATOIE II WINE TABLE IN PIECES   January 1984   Megan Jenkinson

Plate 21
ROBYN KAHUKIWA
He Toa Takitahi
1985
oil and alkyd on canvas
2055mm x 1352mm
The Sarjeant Gallery, Wanganui

He Whakatauki: 'Ehara taku toa i te toa takitahi
Engari he toa takimano no aku tipuna.'
A proverb: 'My strength is not individual, it is collective.'

EHARA, TAKU TOA I TE TOA TAKITAHI ENGARI TAKIMANO NO AKU TIPUNA

Plate 22
EMILY KARAKA
Black Avenger of Prey
1981
oil on jute
1505mm x 940mm
Margaret Crozier, Auckland

The white feather floats,
Aotearoa baton charged
Time on the ground
Watch carefully your measuring piece
Little man, little mortal immoral Man
With blood red mantle over Waikato Aotearoa wakes
Oh Aotearoa; grandmother cries;
Oh Aotearoa
She will rise and eat you up —
Little WHITE Lie
Big BLACK WHITE lie.
AKE   AKE   AKE

Fragment of poem and painting were completed soon after the
last match between the Springboks and the All Blacks at
Eden Park, Auckland, 1981

Plate 23
DORIS LUSK
Canterbury Plains from the Cashmere Hills
1952
oil on textured hardboard
608mm x 1220mm
Robert McDougall Art Gallery, Christchurch

Plate 24
VIVIAN LYNN
The Gates of the Goddess — a Southern Crossing
attended by the Goddess
1983–85
bark cloth, hair, clay, seeds, fibreglass over bamboo armature,
glue colour
2500mm x 4500mm (Goddess panel)
2500mm x 4000mm (side panels)
Auckland City Art Gallery

Plate 25
MOLLY MACALISTER
Cat
1969–70
bronze
170mm
Haydn Family Collection, Auckland

Plate 26
RUHIA OKETOPA (née Reihana)
He tapou harakeke
1970
harekeke — boiled, artificial dyes
4000mm x 2500mm
Ruhia Oketopa Collection, Rotorua

Plate 27
MARIA OLSEN
Embrace
1985
fibreglass, gesso, fabric, pigment, rhoplex
2109mm x 1361mm x (depth) 382mm
Chartwell Collection, Centre for Contemporary Art, Hamilton

Plate 28
GLENDA RANDERSON
Doll's Head with Matisse Painting
1985
oil on canvas
355m x 280mm
Private collection

Plate 29
PUTI HINEAUPOUNAMU RARE (née **Tumohe**)
He mahi taniko
1937
harakeke and traditional dyes
28mm x 18mm
Puti Hineaupounamu Rare Collection, Auckland

Plate 30
PAULINE RHODES
Intensums
1985
steel, wood, board, card, paper, cloth, raffia, grass, wire
Dimensions based on 600mm square units
Height of rods: 1200–1800mm
Dimensions of the two parts: 4200mm diameter circle;
4200mm x 3600mm rectangle
Both parts have extension connecting materials laid on the floor
Temporary installation at Auckland City Art Gallery, 1985

Plate 31
FLORA SCALES
Suburbs outside Paris
1969
oil on canvas
275mm x 350mm
Cohn-Vernon Collection, Auckland

Plate 32
CAROLE SHEPHEARD
John
1981
ceramics, photographs, cast paper
1290mm x 1040mm
The artist

Plate 33
MAY SMITH
Animal Kingdom
1940
lino-cut
325mm x 275mm
Auckland City Art Gallery

Animal Kingdom   MaySmith '40

Plate 34
MARTÉ SZIRMAY
Sculpture for the Gibbs' garden, Auckland
1985
aluminium sheet
1300mm x 1800mm x 1600mm

Plate 35
DIGGERESS RANGITUATAHI TE KANAWA (née Hetet)
He piupiu
1964
Harakeke and traditional dyes
820mm x 630mm
Diggeress Rangituatahi Collection, Te Kuiti

Plate 36
PAULINE THOMPSON
Burning of the Bounty with Tahitian and English Figures
1985
oil on canvas
863mm x 909mm
Roger Donaldson

Plate 37
TEUANE TIBBO
Forceful
c. 1970
acrylic on board
1195mm x 895mm
Graham McGregor, Mt Eden

Plate 38
MERYLYN TWEEDIE
the artist prepares
1985
hand-coloured photograph and ink on paper
335mm x 256mm
Private collection, Auckland

Note: the image is a page in an artist's book.
Text is arranged as follows:
cover: the artist prepares; page 2: the artist prepares;
page 3 (illustrated); page 4: blank; page 5: blank;
page 6: to; page 7: hunt; page 8: blank

Plate 39
LOIS WHITE
On the Air
c. 1935
oil on board
510mm x 405mm
Manawatu Art Gallery, Palmerston North

Plate 40
ROBIN WHITE
A Buzzy Bee for Siulolovao
1977
screenprint
546mm x 267mm

GLOSSARY

ake	upward	muka	fibre from flax
ake, ake, ake	forever	ora	well, alive
hapu	clan or section of tribe	Palagi	(Samoan) foreigner
harakeke	flax	piupiu	flax skirt
huru	feather	poi	ball with string
kai	food	raranga	weaving
kaka	parrot	taha Maori	the Maori way
kakahu	fine clothing	tangata whenua	people of the land, host tribe
karanga	call	tangi	weep, mourn
karanga mate	call of the dead	taniko	ornamental weave
kereru	pigeon	tapa	Pacific bark cloth
kete	basket	tapou	fine mat
kohatu	stone	taro	Pacific root vegetable
kohanga reo	language nest	titi	shearwater
korowai	cloak	tivaevae	Cook Island quilt
kuia	old woman	tukutuku	woven panel work
marae	forecourt in front of meeting house, village common	whare whakairo	meeting house
		whariki	mat
mauri	life principle	whatu	weave